Blerim Burjani

Elections and Reform in Republic of Kosovo

Blerim Burjani

Elections and Reform in Republic of Kosovo

Dictus Publishing

Imprint
Any brand names and product names mentioned in this book are subject to trademark, brand or patent protection and are trademarks or registered trademarks of their respective holders. The use of brand names, product names, common names, trade names, product descriptions etc. even without a particular marking in this work is in no way to be construed to mean that such names may be regarded as unrestricted in respect of trademark and brand protection legislation and could thus be used by anyone.

Cover image: www.ingimage.com

Publisher:
Dictus Publishing
is a trademark of
Dodo Books Indian Ocean Ltd. and OmniScriptum S.R.L publishing group

120 High Road, East Finchley, London, N2 9ED, United Kingdom
Str. Armeneasca 28/1, office 1, Chisinau MD-2012, Republic of Moldova, Europe
Printed at: see last page
ISBN: 978-613-7-35692-0

IKPZH

Blerim Burjani

Elections And Reform in Republic of Kosovo

2023

Abstract

After the war in Kosovo and the arrival of the International Mission - UNMIK based on UNSC Resolution 1244 [1], his mission and all other international mechanisms, including the OSCE, were substantially committed to organizing the Kosovar society from the point of view of the beginning of the functioning of civic and institutional life, after 1999. Kosovo did not have any established institutions that would facilitate normal development of life in Kosovo. The population of Kosovo was scattered around the world, and citizens of Kosovo were progressively returning to Kosovo, the role of the UN Mission was more or less challenging, the functional organization of UNMIK was experienced and UNMIK was assisted by the OSCE, the Council of Europe. In the absence of institutional quorum, the temporary government of Kosovo had appointed temporary mayors of the municipalities in Kosovo. This government was transformed in December 1999, UNMIK established the temporary PISG departments, the political parties had appointed representatives in these departments (PDK, LDK, LBD). up to the organization of elections at both levels.

Keywords: History of elections in Kosovo, ethnic composition of the Assembly, reserved seats, electoral threshold, and electoral reform

1. History of Election in Kosovo

Preparations for the organization of elections

The Civil Administration of the UN, in cooperation with OMiK, created the Joint Registration Task Force (JRT) to register the population of Kosovo [2] , to establish the voting list and to issue identity cards. Approximately one million people from Kosovo were registered.[3] Of them, 38,000 lived outside Kosovo. The registration period also included the certification of 39 political parties, coalitions, civic initiatives and independent candidates for participation in the 2000 municipal elections.[4]

The Central Election Commission (CEC), was founded to determine the rules governing the elections, consisted of nine people from Kosovo and was chaired by the Presidency of OMiK. The CEC successfully separated the technical from the political in the election preparations. The CEC acted as the main regulatory body to oversee the smooth running and supervision of the

---

[1] Misioni Ndërkombëtar - UNMIK bazuar në Rezolutën 1244 të KS të OKB pë themelimin IPVQ.

[2] Daan Everst, **Review of the OSCE mission in Kosovo's activities 1999-2001,**
https://reliefweb.int/report/serbia/revieë-osce-mission-kosovos-activities-1999-2001

[3] Daan Everst, **Review of the OSCE mission in Kosovo's activities 1999-2001,**
https://reliefweb.int/report/serbia/revieë-osce-mission-kosovos-activities-1999-2001

[4] Daan Everst, **Review of the OSCE mission in Kosovo's activities 1999-2001,**
https://reliefëeb.int/report/serbia/revieë-osce-mission-kosovos-activities-1999-2001

electoral process; while extensive consultations on the decisions made by the CEC took place within the newly established Political Parties Consultative Forum (PPCF).[5]

The same was true for the Electoral Commission for Complaints and Submissions (KZAP) which ensured that political violations were kept to a minimum by issuing harsh penalties for violations of the Code of Electoral Conduct..[6]

At the municipal level, the Municipal Election Commissions and Polling Stations were created. As part of OMiK's capacity building mandate, special emphasis has been placed on the progressive transfer of electoral expertise to local professionals. Candidate training was also an essential part of the OSCE's election preparations. Political parties were trained in the need to adapt to new requirements for transparency, financial and programmatic accountability and electoral codes of conduct, media rules, etc. Given the requirement that every third candidate on the party list be a woman, a special focus was given to the training of women candidates.[7]

1.1. Establishment of the Political Party Consultative Forum

OMiK to facilitate the organization of the first democratic and free elections established the Consultative Forum of Political Parties in Kosovo, all parties sent representatives to this forum to give their views on the electoral system, the discussions were led by Ambassador Daan Everts from the OSCE. The Consultative Forum of Political Parties discussed the system that will be used at both levels of elections in Kosovo, discussions were held almost every week with the aim of improving the participation of the electoral system, by FKPP (Consultative Forum of Political Parties)[8], Ambassador Dann Everts about the determination of the proportional system for the two levels had drawn the following conclusion: It is believed that the selection of the proportional system encouraged a more moderate political climate, prevented the formation of a bipolar political reality and ensured small and minority parties to achieve some fairer representation, the same reasoning applied when OMiK recommended that a system of proportional representation be incorporated into the Constitutional Framework, which will, among other things, determine the electoral formula for the Kosovo-wide elections scheduled for November 2001.[9]

---

[5] Daan Everst, **Review of the OSCE mission in Kosovo's activities 1999-2001,**
https://reliefweb.int/report/serbia/revieë-osce-mission-kosovos-activities-1999-2001
[6] Daan Everst, **Review of the OSCE mission in Kosovo's activities 1999-2001,**
https://reliefëeb.int/report/serbia/revieë-osce-mission-kosovos-activities-1999-2001
[7] Daan Everst, **Review of the OSCE mission in Kosovo's activities 1999-2001,**
https://reliefëeb.int/report/serbia/revieë-osce-mission-kosovos-activities-1999-2001
[8] Forumi Konsultative I Partive Politike kishte vendos dialogun nderpartiak me OSBE
[9] Daan Everst, **Review of the OSCE mission in Kosovo's activities 1999-2001,**
https://reliefweb.int/report/serbia/revieë-osce-mission-kosovos-activities-1999-2001

So it was a conclusion that the proportional system should also be included in the Constitutional Framework of Kosovo and later it was decided in the Constitution of the Republic of Kosovo after the declaration of independence on February 17, 2008. Congress of Local and Regional Authorities of Europe.[10],had said from the beginning that the elections should be based on the legislation that regulates the functioning of the municipalities, which finally thanks to the signing by Bernard Kouchner of Regulation no. 2000/45 on the self-government of municipalities in Kosovo in July 2000, the conditions and reasons for holding elections were created. Although this Regulation does not meet the expectation of the Congress in all points, especially since the municipalities will not have their own resources at this initial stage, it was nevertheless an attempt to get as close as possible to European standards, and it is specifically referred to in the preamble of the European Charter of Local Self-Government, as one of its sources of inspiration. Congressional experts have regularly assisted in the preparation of this text.[11]

In this way, some conditions were fulfilled to start the phase of institutional and democratic construction in Kosovo. OMiK has supported and facilitated the electoral process since the beginning of the campaign or the pre-election campaign from September 13, 2000, the suggestions were that the campaign should be oriented towards local and economic issues, since those elections were at the municipal level and that the campaign of the political parties should to be oriented is the development of local services for citizens and economic issues, however, this area was developed by dealing with general national rather than local issues, despite the fact that the OSCE conceived the "Voices of Voters" project, to help the parties political to address local community concerns related to vital local issues, water, sanitation, transportation, environment and others, this concept was designed to encourage political parties and candidates to focus on concrete and specific issues. However, the parties' campaign was more of a character for national problems. The concept of OMiK helped the parties to run the campaign for the benefit of the electorate, so the concept gave a tool with which the parties would engage their political candidates in discussions and debates related to local issues. The concept of OMiK "Voters Voices" informed the Kosovo electorate about the issues of importance in an electoral municipality, while the Voter Education Campaign informed the population about the electoral system.[12]

All the participating political parties had agreed that every third woman should be on the electoral list of political subjects, so the quota was 33% of the electoral list to be made up of women to respect the equality to some extent of the participation of female candidates, this sounded during the discussions in the forum of political parties that there was and still is

---

[10] **Observations of the Congress of Local and Regional Authorities of Europe**https://rm.coe.int/168071a3cf, kane vwzhguar zgjedhjet locale tw vitit 2000

[11] Daan Everst, Review of the OSCE mission in Kosovo's activities 1999-2001, https://reliefweb.int/report/serbia/revieë-osce-mission-kosovos-activities-1999-2001

[12] Daan Everst, Review of the OSCE mission in Kosovo's activities 1999-2001, https://reliefweb.int/report/serbia/review-osce-mission-kosovos-activities-1999-2001

discrimination against women in political and institutional life, and that ensuring the presence of female contestants should be administratively placed on the list. However, only 8% of the candidates actually elected were women. During the pre-election period and throughout the campaign period, OMiK ensured equal access to the media from all political entities. All media were asked to provide time for political spots and debates. Donor support enabled OMiK to establish a media fund to support the production of these political announcements. A network of regionally based teams monitored compliance with election rules on media access; panels of local citizens and international experts investigated and referred complaints to the CEC or the Interim Commissioner for Media.[13]

On election day, turnout was almost 80%, and the percentage of invalid votes was extremely low (3.4%).[14]. Surprisingly, the day was virtually without security incidents. [15] The Serbs had boycotted the local elections previously organized by the international community, although Bernard Kuchner had promised to create favorable conditions for the Serbian minority to participate in the local elections, the political and ethnic atmosphere and Serbia at that time had a negative impact so that the Kosovar Serbs would not participate in the elections. The previous elections, organized with full international assistance, were considered successful, what characterizes the local elections of October 28, 2000 was the massive participation of citizens, high-level civil discipline, as well as the interest of citizens to participate in these elections. the massive participation of citizens in the 80% turnout quota, never happened again in subsequent elections and until today in the state of Kosovo. The Local Elections of 2000 can be defined as historic elections in a country under construction to a new local democracy.

1.2.Constitutional framework and seats reserved for minorities

The Constitutional Framework was a preliminary framework which would regulate the institutional and democratic functioning of Kosovo in the transitional period until the definition of the political status of Kosovo, the constitutional framework had enabled minorities in the electoral process to have reserved seats in the Assembly and the composition of the government it is also multi-ethnic. According to this framework, the Assembly of Kosovo had 120 seats, 100 seats will be elected by the majority of the Albanian population, while 10 seats are reserved for the Serbian minority community, ten (10) seats are allocated to other communities as follows : the Roma,

---

[13] Daan Everst, Review of the OSCE mission in Kosovo's activities 1999-2001,

https://reliefweb.int/report/serbia/revieë-osce-mission-kosovos-activities-1999-2001

[14] Daan Everst, Revieë of the OSCE mission in Kosovo's activities 1999-2001,

https://reliefweb.int/report/serbia/revieë-osce-mission-kosovos-activities-1999-2001

[15] Daan Everst, Revieë of the OSCE mission in Kosovo's activities 1999-2001,

https://reliefweb.int/report/serbia/revieë-osce-mission-kosovos-activities-1999-2001

the Ashkali and the Egyptian community four (4), the Bosnian community three (3), the Turkish c The Constitution of the Republic of Kosovo - regarding the structure of the assembly in Article 64 specifies as follows: "within this division: twenty (20) one hundred out of (120) seats are guaranteed for the representation of communities that are not the majority in Kosovo. The reserved seats, even though there was no need to exist, the constitutional framework saw them as necessary, even though in the formal, practical institutional aspect, there was no importance that any ethnic political benefit would happen in the future, despite the hopes of the minorities that it might happen. that through reserved places, minorities can have a larger number of representatives of minorities in the Assembly in any created situation remains only hope. The list of parties that had to include women every third candidate in the electoral list was assured that there will be no discrimination against women, but the government does not respect this representative solution as in the Assembly to be in the Government, no prime minister until today since the parliamentary elections from 2001 decided as an obligation that the Government as well as the Assembly of Kosovo should have a representative role of women in the government around 33%.ommunity two (2) and the Goran community one.[16]

There have been complaints from male candidates about the distribution of seats in the Municipal Assemblies and at the central level in the Assembly, and there have also been many televised debates favoring the fact that this representative quota for women in institutions should remain. Other topics along this history of the development of electoral democracy was the topic of the electoral threshold, small parties that do not have representatives in the Assembly are currently insisting that the electoral threshold be reduced to 3% (NISMA).[17], Movement for Unity), while other major parties do not see the electoral threshold of 5% as a problem to discuss and change. Let us remind that the electoral threshold is not regulated by law. Reducing the electoral threshold would be even more complicated because the formation of central institutions would be more heterogeneous and more problematic to govern due to the fragmentation of responsibility, the lack of accountability, the history of the government that until the last election wins VV over 50%[18] to vote, it was a misuse of the state budget, the corruption developed in the government and the loss of responsibility to the citizens, so the idea to reduce the electoral threshold is more of an idea for even smaller parties to become part of the government, so more there is damage earlier in the misuse of the budget due to multi-party governments than the efficiency of the government, the then prime ministers could not dismiss the ministers with poor

---

[16] Per me teper shih :Kornizen Kushtetuse tw Kosovws nenin 9.1.2,9.1.3 ,pika a dhe b., http://old.kuvendikosoves.org/common/docs/FrameworkPocket_ALB_Dec2002.pdf,20.05.2022

[17] **Çka ndodh nëse ulet pragu zgjedhor?** Socialdemokrate, Fatmir Limaj, ka kërkuar që pragu prej 5 për qind të ulet në 2 ose 3 për qind, https://www.syri.net/syri_kosova/lajme/373622/cka-ndodh-nese-ulet-pragu-zgjedhor/, **6/05/2022**

[18] **Zgjedhjet parlamentare në Kosovë, 2021,** https://sq.wikipedia.org/wiki/Zgjedhjet_parlamentare_n%C3%AB_Kosov%C3%AB,_2021,26.05.2022

performance from the parties in the coalition or due to the misuse of the minister's position. The governments of 2001, 2017 consisted of many ministries up to 19 ministries, which happened because the winning party or coalition could not form the government only by the number of votes in the Assembly, it was forced to make political agreements with partners of the winning coalition, to increase the number of ministries and to accommodate one of them in the executive body.

1.3. List open / closed

Open proportional lists were applied for the first time in the local elections of October 28, 2000. In the 27th parliamentary elections in November 2001, the closed list of the proportional system was applied, which reflected more positivity in terms of the rules of the electoral process, there was less manipulation and theft of votes, the lists were opened as a result of the complaints given to me by the civil society but also by the political parties in order to enable the citizens to choose freely who they want. In the closed list, the ranking of the candidates was mostly done by the party leader, the cooperation of the party leader or party leader with the branches of the parties in the field was very weak, this resulted in the opening of the electoral list to vote for the candidate on the open list and for the good of the citizen to choose whomever he wants to represent him in the Assembly

What was learned from the history of the organization of elections in the state of Kosovo

The closed electoral list is less democratic but does not produce misuse and theft of votes between candidates of the same party, the closed list had its shortcomings but the management of the elections was more stable and effective, without problems and much less complaints and administrative and judicial procedures, the delay in the certification of election results has happened and still happens today, because the open list in the proportional system produces more complaints than the closed list, the procedure for recounting the votes of candidates, as a result of complaints that exercise candidates of political parties at both election levels, the procedures are followed in the courts and this complicates to a considerable extent the final certification of the elections, sometimes such a delay is considered to be close to the conclusion of the elections, this has caused many international and local observers to have many comments and remarks and recommendations for electoral reform. The open proportional list remains absolute so far desired by all parties and their candidates for elections at both levels, another characteristic can be drawn that even the candidates of the political parties have not trust in the party they belong to when it comes to the normal process of winning votes from elections, for this reason party candidates support the open proportional system, because they trust the citizens more than the party they belong to when it comes to the votes won from the electorate. Political parties in the closed proportional list, even though their party commissioners count the votes, the possibilities of stealing votes or abusing the position of the vote counter in the name of the party they belong to are completely small, so there is no misuse or theft for because each party counts the votes of its party, and according to the percentage won and how the candidates on the list are weighted from the leader who usually leads the list, to the last candidate in percentage who won the political party, so there is no problem, this list produces uncontested deputies as long as the list is open produces winners many times contested by candidates from the same party, usually accused of stealing votes and support of the commissioners from the same party, as long as the 25,000 female commissioners of the parties can steal votes for a certain candidate, this causes a serious problem, until today there were convictions for problematic commissioners, but Kosovo continues to have problems of its own nature , this phenomenon must be stopped by changing the law and electoral rules by replacing vote counting commissioners with civil servants, if civil servants make manipulations they lose their jobs, so the caution is many times the greatest of not committing criminal offenses from elections.

1.4. Electoral Zone

Since the one electoral zone system was decided in Kosovo, there has been no agreement from the political parties to approve more electoral zones, even though it is actually more democratic to have more electoral zones, where each electoral zone produces a certain number of deputies. normally this would be much more democratic, but so far there is no consensus from the political parties to approve more zones by consensus, my opinion was that Kosovo could have 6-7 electoral zones, there are political parties that have requested that Kosovo have 100 electoral zones (AAK), other parties have requested much fewer electoral zones. The correct geo-geographic territorial representation of the citizens is impossible in the single electoral district system. There is no great hope that the political parties will agree or reach a consensus on the division into more electoral zones. So, in reality, the one-zone system is a convenient system for all political parties, as well as the proportional system, which at least offers a hope. great that as many parties cross the electoral threshold, so the chances are very minimal in changing the electoral system.

1.5. Voting List

There are always problems regarding the cleaning of the voting list, despite the great efforts of the Ministry of Internal Affairs in cooperation (2010) with the CEC, not so much progress has been achieved, the problems continue to remain the same, although until today there are gradual improvements, but the problem of cleaning the voter list is still a challenge in meeting ODIR or EC standards. Legal basis of elections At the meeting of the Assembly of Kosovo on June 6, 2008, two basic laws were approved for the organization of elections in the Republic of Kosovo, the Law on General Elections and the Law on Local Elections. While the election rules were approved after the issuance of the laws, let us recall that the rules elections have remained since the time of the international administration of elections in Kosovo, the CEC has approved the election rules.

Chronological history of the organization of elections in the Republic of Kosovo

	Parliamentary elections in Kosovo	
1	Parliamentary elections in Kosovo	2001
2	Parliamentary elections in Kosovo	2004
3	Parliamentary elections in Kosovo	2007
4	Parliamentary elections in Kosovo	2010
5	Parliamentary elections in Kosovo	2014
6	Parliamentary elections in Kosovo	2017
7	Parliamentary elections in Kosovo	2019
8	Parliamentary elections in Kosovo	2021

	Elections for Municipal Assemblies	
1	Elections for Municipal Assemblies	2000
2	Elections for Municipal Assemblies	2002
3	Elections for Municipal Assemblies	2007
4	Elections for Municipal Assemblies	2009
5	Elections for Municipal Assemblies	2010
6	Elections for Municipal Assemblies	2013
7	Elections for Municipal Assemblies	2017
8	Elections for Municipal Assemblies	2021

2.Challenges of Election Administration in Kosovo

Elections in the Republic of Kosovo are still a challenge that stems from not changing and not reforming the election law. So far, many observers have made recommendations among themselves EU Observers, the Council of Europe, but without change and without impact towards a reform. Political parties in Kosovo do not have the will to change anything in the electoral process, they are used to working with this legal infrastructure that I assess suits them. The control of electoral mechanisms with the nominees from political parties suits them. The challenges will continue as they are until there is a reform that in my opinion should be electoral and electoral system.

During the work I will use the analytical, descriptive, comparative and empirical methodology.

2.1. Defining the problem

Kosovo has a proportional electoral system with open lists, and Kosovo is only an electoral constituency, so Kosovo is not divided into several constituencies and this is one of the problems regarding the representation of all regions through MPs. Political parties when competing at the level Nationals do not compile a list of deputies where the regions are democratically represented, so it happens that one city has many deputies competing and other cities remain without a candidate. This is the case with political composition, political parties do not accurately declare donors and revenues, even despite the audit of revenues and the fact that the audit company is elected by the CEC, they still do not conduct an independent audit.

Furthermore, the Law on Political Parties does not define what happens if a political party violates the state constitution? Or acts against the constitution of the state. The other problem and the other main challenge is the CEC, the MEC and the PSC are politically composed, which is reflected in many irregularities during the general election process starting with the CEC as the organizer of the elections, the composition of the MEC and the PSC, these three mechanisms are active problems related to the administration of elections in Kosovo, decision-making in all these electoral mechanisms is political and is led by the parties that make up these electoral institutions, starting with the nomination of CEC members, the nomination of Municipal Election Commissions and the Polling Station Councils that count votes and manipulate and steal votes of their candidates within the same political party in the open proportional list. So there are three factors that have prompted me to draft this paper, in order to contribute to the amendment of the Law on General Elections in the Republic of Kosovo. The first factor is the ineffective administration of elections through n is the open proportional electoral system by the CEC, the second factor is the legal reform of the existing legal system, and the third factor is the depoliticization of the electoral mechanisms as follows: CEC, MEC and PSC. So the main challenges are the administration of elections when this process is controlled by political parties and directly affect the organization of elections through electoral institutions CEC, MEC and PSC, all three of these institutions pose the greatest challenge for Kosovo to organize elections with high standards of ODIR.

Therefore, the purpose of this paper is to depoliticize these institutions that negatively affect the organizational and technical process of elections in Kosovo. So the main challenges are the administration of elections when this process is controlled by political parties and directly affect the organization of elections through electoral institutions CEC, MEC and PSC, all three of these institutions pose the greatest challenge for Kosovo to organize elections with high ODIR standards.

The purpose of this paper is to reform legal electoral system respectively   managerial bodies such is CEC, MEC-s, PSC

12

2,2 Central Election Commission (CEC)

The CEC is a permanent independent body composed of eleven members. The Chairperson is appointed by the President of Kosovo from among the judges of the Supreme Court. The ten other members of the CEC are appointed through nominations by parliamentary groups represented in the Assembly, including those holding guaranteed seats for non-majority communities.[19]

The CEC is called independent by Article 139 of the State Constitution[20], but the political groups in the Assembly of Kosovo appoint their representatives to the CEC, this has caused complete dependence of the CEC members who are nominated by parties or parliamentary groups in the Assembly of Kosovo.

Elections in the Republic of Kosovo are not infrequently managerial challenges, the whole process of election administration depends on the Central Election Commission, while the Law on Local Elections and General Elections talk about local electoral mechanisms such as Municipal Election Councils and Local Councils. are two important electoral mechanisms. The electoral process in Kosovo is decentralized and managed by the CEC, as a key institution and responsible for electoral organization and administration.

2.3. Findings of observers

The appointment of 2,505 PSCs and their chairpersons was a complex process. The PSCs consisted normally of five to seven members.[21] The mechanism for the establishment of the PSCs gave the right for nominations to the political entities represented in the Kosovo Assembly and the political entities with seats in the respective Municipal Assembly contesting in the elections.[22] One political entity was allowed to have only one member in a PSC and thus the CEC allocated quotas for the number of PSC members, reserves and chairpersons for each political entity within each municipality,[23] The main issue was to equally divide the number of PSC chairpersons among the four political entities that received most of the votes in the 2017 legislative elections in the respective municipality. The CEC adopted quotas for the number of PSC chairpersons thus maintaining an inclusive and balanced approach for the PSC composition in all municipalities incorporating various contesting political

---

[19]Election Observation and Democracy Support EODS, http: //www.eods. eu/library/final report kosovo english 0.pdf,

[20] Constitution of Republic of Kosovo, Article 139

[21] KOSOVO* MAYORAL AND MUNICIPAL ASSEMBLY ELECTIONS, EUROPEAN UNION ELECTION OBSERVATION MISSION, FINAL REPORT, 22 OCTOBER 2017

[22] KOSOVO* MAYORAL AND MUNICIPAL ASSEMBLY ELECTIONS, EUROPEAN UNION ELECTION OBSERVATION MISSION , FINAL REPORT, 22 OCTOBER 2017

[23] KOSOVO* MAYORAL AND MUNICIPAL ASSEMBLY ELECTIONS, EUROPEAN UNION ELECTION OBSERVATION MISSION , FINAL REPORT, 22 OCTOBER 2017

entities representing the Kosovo Serb and other nonmajority communities. For the second round of the mayoral elections, the CEC appointed the PSC members attributing an equal number of chairperson positions to the two competing political entities in each municipality, which faced a runoff. As for the other PSC member positions, political entities had the right to confirm or replace their polling staff from the first round. Some political parties replaced their PSC members accordingly.[24]

The spirit of cooperation between CEC members has been violated in several cases, related to the decision regarding valid identification documents, the composition of MECs and PSCs, the voting operation abroad and the like.[25] Almost all meetings held by the CEC have been announced to the public, and most of the approved documents or materials have been provided. In this regard, the CEC has made significant progress in terms of transparency and cooperation with stakeholders, especially with local civil society organizations.[26] The relatively high number of invalid ballots, which in these elections is about 4%, ie 33,271 of them, of which 12,374 were empty, is a clear indicator that informing the public about the electoral process, in particular about voting procedures is not has been at an adequate level. In addition to technical reasons, the short period for informing and educating voters, especially for young voters and other groups that should be a priority of the CEC, has also contributed to the failure to provide proper and targeted information to the public.[27] The CEC, through a closed negotiated tender procedure, has selected an external company to manage the voter information and education component. As in previous elections, TV spots have appeared on the public broadcaster and other media.[28] The CEC, in the campaign for information and education of voters in the elections of October 6, 2019, in addition to traditional media has also used social networks. However, the CEC has not shown an interactive approach to the public, although social media is conceived as two-way

---

[24] KOSOVO* MAYORAL AND MUNICIPAL ASSEMBLY ELECTIONS, EUROPEAN UNION ELECTION OBSERVATION MISSION , FINAL REPORT, 22 OCTOBER 2017
[25] Raporti I Vezhgimit te Zgjedhjeve, Zgjedhjet për Kuvendin e Kosovës, http://demokracianeveprim.org/wp-content/uploads/2019/12/DnV_RAPORTI-I-V%C3%8BZHGIMIT-T%C3%8B-ZGJEDHJEVE.pdf,2019, pp 16
[26] Raporti I Vezhgimit te Zgjedhjeve, Zgjedhjet për Kuvendin e Kosovës, http://demokracianeveprim.org/wp-content/uploads/2019/12/DnV_RAPORTI-I-V%C3%8BZHGIMIT-T%C3%8B-ZGJEDHJEVE.pdf,2019,pp16
[27] Raporti I Vezhgimit te Zgjedhjeve, Zgjedhjet për Kuvendin e Kosovës, http://demokracianeveprim.org/wp-content/uploads/2019/12/DnV_RAPORTI-I-V%C3%8BZHGIMIT-T%C3%8B-ZGJEDHJEVE.pdf,2019,pp18
[28] Raporti I Vezhgimit te Zgjedhjeve, Zgjedhjet për Kuvendin e Kosovës, http://demokracianeveprim.org/wp-content/uploads/2019/12/DnV_RAPORTI-I-V%C3%8BZHGIMIT-T%C3%8B-ZGJEDHJEVE.pdf,2019,pp18

communication.[29] Also, no suitable products have been created specifically for a communication channel.[30]

In the framework of the administration of the electoral process, it is worth mentioning the case of loss of 450 ballots in the polling station 2114B / 01R in the municipality of Skënderaj.[31] As a result of the issuance of these ballots outside the polling station, the ECAP initially decided to ban the participation of all PSC members in question and other observers present.[32] This issue had also caused problems during the processing of data in the CRC, as the polling station in question could not be processed as regular, due to the lack of ballot papers in the box and the inability to pass the audit process.[33] For this reason, in one of its meetings, the CEC, after | 19 recommendation from the CRC, had decided to increase the level of tolerance of ballot discrepancies in - + 450 polling stations in question, so that the results are accepted as regular and included in the final results.[34]

Municipal Election Commissions and Polling Station Councils The appointment of Municipal Election Commissions (MECs) has encountered difficulties during this election process.[35] The decision on the appointment of MEC members was taken in accordance with the deadlines in the operational plan, according to which the appointment of MECs was scheduled to end on 4 September. Despite numerous disagreements over the formula for the composition of commissions between CEC members from the ruling and opposition parties, the CEC had approved the decision to appoint members to all municipalities, including nominations by political entities which have competed within a single entity in the last parliamentary elections. Members from the ranks of political entities in opposition (LDK and LVV) had demanded that the division formula be based on the LPZ, which requires members to be nominated only by political entities that have run in elections and have crossed the threshold. In

---

[29] Raporti I Vezhgimit te Zgjedhjeve, Zgjedhjet për Kuvendin e Kosovës, http://demokracianeveprim.org/wp-content/uploads/2019/12/DnV_RAPORTI-I-V%C3%8BZHGIMIT-T%C3%8B-ZGJEDHJEVE.pdf,2019,pp18

[30] Raporti I Vezhgimit te Zgjedhjeve, Zgjedhjet për Kuvendin e Kosovës, http://demokracianeveprim.org/wp-content/uploads/2019/12/DnV_RAPORTI-I-V%C3%8BZHGIMIT-T%C3%8B-ZGJEDHJEVE.pdf,2019,pp18

[31] Raporti I Vezhgimit te Zgjedhjeve, Zgjedhjet për Kuvendin e Kosovës, http://demokracianeveprim.org/wp-content/uploads/2019/12/DnV_RAPORTI-I-V%C3%8BZHGIMIT-T%C3%8B-ZGJEDHJEVE.pdf,2019,pp18

[32] Raporti I Vezhgimit te Zgjedhjeve, Zgjedhjet për Kuvendin e Kosovës, http://demokracianeveprim.org/wp-content/uploads/2019/12/DnV_RAPORTI-I-V%C3%8BZHGIMIT-T%C3%8B-ZGJEDHJEVE.pdf,2019,pp18

[33] Raporti I Vezhgimit te Zgjedhjeve, Zgjedhjet për Kuvendin e Kosovës, http://demokracianeveprim.org/wp-content/uploads/2019/12/DnV_RAPORTI-I-V%C3%8BZHGIMIT-T%C3%8B-ZGJEDHJEVE.pdf,2019,pp18

[34] Raporti I Vezhgimit te Zgjedhjeve, Zgjedhjet për Kuvendin e Kosovës, http://demokracianeveprim.org/wp-content/uploads/2019/12/DnV_RAPORTI-I-V%C3%8BZHGIMIT-T%C3%8B-ZGJEDHJEVE.pdf,2019,pp18

[35] Raporti I Vezhgimit te Zgjedhjeve, Zgjedhjet për Kuvendin e Kosovës, http://demokracianeveprim.org/wp-content/uploads/2019/12/DnV_RAPORTI-I-V%C3%8BZHGIMIT-T%C3%8B-ZGJEDHJEVE.pdf,2019,pp18

municipalities with distinct numbers of non-majority communities, MECs reflected the demographic composition of the respective municipalities.[36]
Some of the issues that have accompanied the process of compiling the Final Voters List have been related to the inclusion of deceased persons, but also the non-inclusion of voters who have recently issued documents of the Republic of Kosovo.[37]
Voting from abroad, conducted by mail, has been described as one of the most sensitive and problematic issues in this election.[38] This process has been accompanied by challenges, which have also affected the integrity of the electoral process.[39] The packages with supposed ballots that arrived late from abroad, as well as the organized way of transporting the packages from Serbia, are the two main issues that have characterized this process [40]

2,4. Municipal Election Commissions

The appointment of Municipal Election Commissions (MECs) has encountered difficulties during this election process. [41]The decision on the appointment of MEC members was taken in accordance with the deadlines in the operational plan, according to which the appointment of MECs was scheduled to end on 4 September.[42] Despite numerous disagreements over the formula for the composition of commissions between CEC members from the ruling and opposition parties, the CEC had approved the decision to appoint members to all municipalities, including nominations by political entities which have competed within a single entity in the last parliamentary elections. Members from the ranks of political entities in opposition (LDK and LVV) had demanded that the division formula be based on the LPZ, which requires members to be nominated only by political entities that have run in elections and have crossed the

---

[36] Raporti I Vezhgimit te Zgjedhjeve, Zgjedhjet për Kuvendin e Kosovës, http://demokracianeveprim.org/wp-content/uploads/2019/12/DnV_RAPORTI-I-V%C3%8BZHGIMIT-T%C3%8B-ZGJEDHJEVE.pdf,2019,pp19

[37] Raporti I Vezhgimit te Zgjedhjeve, Zgjedhjet për Kuvendin e Kosovës, http://demokracianeveprim.org/wp-content/uploads/2019/12/DnV_RAPORTI-I-V%C3%8BZHGIMIT-T%C3%8B-ZGJEDHJEVE.pdf,2019,pp23

[38] Raporti I Vezhgimit te Zgjedhjeve, Zgjedhjet për Kuvendin e Kosovës, http://demokracianeveprim.org/wp-content/uploads/2019/12/DnV_RAPORTI-I-V%C3%8BZHGIMIT-T%C3%8B-ZGJEDHJEVE.pdf,2019,pp23

[39] Raporti I Vezhgimit te Zgjedhjeve, Zgjedhjet për Kuvendin e Kosovës, http://demokracianeveprim.org/wp-content/uploads/2019/12/DnV_RAPORTI-I-V%C3%8BZHGIMIT-T%C3%8B-ZGJEDHJEVE.pdf,2019,pp23

[40] Raporti I Vezhgimit te Zgjedhjeve, Zgjedhjet për Kuvendin e Kosovës, http://demokracianeveprim.org/wp-content/uploads/2019/12/DnV_RAPORTI-I-V%C3%8BZHGIMIT-T%C3%8B-ZGJEDHJEVE.pdf,2019,pp23

[41] Raporti I Vezhgimit te Zgjedhjeve, Zgjedhjet për Kuvendin e Kosovës, http://demokracianeveprim.org/wp-content/uploads/2019/12/DnV_RAPORTI-I-V%C3%8BZHGIMIT-T%C3%8B-ZGJEDHJEVE.pdf,2019,pp19

[42] Raporti I Vezhgimit te Zgjedhjeve, Zgjedhjet për Kuvendin e Kosovës, http://demokracianeveprim.org/wp-content/uploads/2019/12/DnV_RAPORTI-I-V%C3%8BZHGIMIT-T%C3%8B-ZGJEDHJEVE.pdf,2019,pp19

threshold. In municipalities with distinct numbers of non-majority communities, MECs reflected the demographic composition of the respective municipalities. [43]

3.What are the challenges of the process?

3.1. Decision-making at the CEC is politicized because this institution consists of political party nominees; the election certification process has so far been difficult to follow due to the influence of political parties through their nominees at the CEC. Decision-making is very complex.

3.2. Municipal Election Commissions (MECs)

The commissions are composed of political parties and often there are many problems, especially the election of MEC chairpersons, its decision-making is also reflected by the political parties that make up the Kosovo Assembly and Municipal Assemblies. Parties and Civic Initiatives that can compete in one of these levels as a new party have no representatives in the MEC.
The MEC should be composed of civil servants in the future, ie it should be fully politicized because it offers more independent and neutral opportunities to manage the election process in an effective and impartial and equal manner for all political parties running in the elections.

3.3. Polling Station Councils and Ballot Counting

The challenges of the process are the counting of the votes of the candidates of the political parties, while for the counting of the votes of the parties does not present any serious challenge, so far, the managerial practice has shown that the main problem remains the counting of the votes of the candidates.

The biggest challenge so far is the counting of votes by the commissioners of the parties participating in the counting of the votes of their party members in the open electoral list of the proportional system, including the number of votes of the party.

This has led many candidates to complain to the ECAP [44] (Appeals Review Body), to the Constitutional Court and to the Supreme Court.

 Counting the votes of political party candidates is one of the main problems that tarnishes the image of the elections, damages the electoral integrity and causes great trouble then in verifying the votes won by the candidates of political parties. This problem remains chronic since 2000 when for the first-time local elections were

---

[43] Raporti I Vezhgimit te Zgjedhjeve, Zgjedhjet për Kuvendin e Kosovës, http://demokracianeveprim.org/wp-content/uploads/2019/12/DnV_RAPORTI-I-V%C3%8BZHGIMIT-T%C3%8B-ZGJEDHJEVE.pdf,2019,pp19
[44] Commission for Election Complaints and Appeals Panel (ECAP)

organized in the Republic of Kosovo with similar problems manipulation continued in the parliamentary elections in 2004[45], 2007[46], 2010[47], 2013[48], 2014[49], 2017[50] ,2019[51].

Observation missions in Kosovo, especially after 2008, were more recommended and more critical than when UNMIK was the interim administrator of Kosovo. During these years, there were almost always remarks, recommendations, requests to improve the work of successful organization and administration of elections.

 The problems are almost very different from the international reports, but what is missing is the immediate reform that should have happened, Kosovo so far has not even managed even slowly to improve the electoral legal structure and also lacks the reform of elected rules as I said Many times in numerous televised debates and roundtables with civil society, as a CEC member I have made continuous efforts to reform the law on elections at both levels. To have an ongoing voter list update, to depoliticize the electoral mechanisms in Kosovo The first attempts at electoral reform were in 2005 involving the OSCE, IFES and others a, but something could not be corrected in the electoral system, this roundtable was held in May 2005.With high pressure from civil society and international mechanisms the proportional list was opened and voting was done for the party and for the party candidate, this resulted in more irregularities in the 2007 elections, there were full candidates dissatisfied with the number of votes.

 In 2010, the Ad-hoc Commission was established by the Assembly of Kosovo, but even this commission failed to reform the electoral system. At that time, as a CEC member, I sent a 20 -page document on legal changes and amendments, as well I provide my recommendations to change electoral law . This Parliamentary Commission composed of political parties failed to reform electoral system. To date no substantial reform has

---

[45] Council of Europe , Observation Mission KOSOVO, General Election, October 2004, https://reliefweb.int/report/serbia/observation-assembly-elections-kosovo-october-2004,
[46] Council of Europe , Observation Mission KOSOVO V,CEEOM,5 October – 5 December 2007
[47] European Union Election Observation Mission KOSOVO, ELECTION OBSERVATION DELEGATION TO THE GENERAL ELECTION IN KOSOVO (12 December 2010, 9 January 2011)
[48]European Union Election Observation Mission KOSOVO, KOSOVO* MUNICIPAL ELECTIONS 3 NOVEMBER AND 1 DECEMBER 2013 FINAL REPORT JANUARY 2014,
[49] The European Union Election Observation Mission (EU EOM), KOSOVO1 LEGISLATIVE ELECTIONS 8 JUNE 2014, https://eeas.europa.eu/archives/eueom/missions/2014/kosovo/pdf/eu-eom-kosovo-2014-final-report_en.pdf,1.11.2020
[50] The European Union Election Observation Mission (EU EOM) to Kosovo presented its Final Report on the 11 June 2017 legislative elections today. The report comprises an assessment of the electoral process and offers 26 recommendations to improve future electoral processes in Kosovo, 12.09.2017
[51] European Union Election Observation Mission KOSOVO 2019 Final Report.Report of 6 October 2019 . This Report contains to some extent the same recommendations as in previous reports. For more details see Report: http://www.epgencms.europarl.europa.eu/cmsdata/upload/1e4f1465-9cdd-4565-a837-a0487b092e51/Kosovo_early-legislative-elections_6-October-2019_final-report.pdf, 20.11.2020
10Ad.Hoc Parliamentary Commission, For Electoral Reform, February 2010.
11 Blerim Burjani, Member of Central Election Commission (CEC), May , 2010

been made, the problems remain the same, the laws remain the same and fewer changes to the electoral rules.

In the elections of October 6, 2019, a mess was created around the crossing of the electoral threshold of the NISMA party; the certification process of these elections had taken about three months from the end of the elections. The counting of votes shows that the Social Democratic Initiative had not crossed the electoral threshold based on the announcement of the preliminary results by the CEC[52]. The turnout of the citizens of the state of Kosovo was 44.18%, a total of 812 thousand and 49 voters voted.

.3.Necessary amendments to the Law on General Elections of the Republic of Kosovo

4. Research findings

Article 11.1 of the Law on General Elections should be amended

which refers to the establishment of the Office for Registration of Political Parties, so my opinion is that this article should be amended and that the registration of political parties should be done in the judiciary, political parties cannot exert influence or pressure on the judiciary, in case when political parties violate the Constitution, will be deregistered from the register of political parties (model of other countries and the region, Slovenia , Montenegro, Serbia, Bosnia and Herzegovina, Croatia, etc.

The law should strictly prohibit the pre-campaign of political parties, especially after the announcement of elections, whether at the parliamentary or local level. This area is not regulated by law and is being misused by political parties. Article 37 which refers to the recognition of election results of political parties states that parties are obliged to accept and implement election results after certification of results by the CEC, but does not say what other legal measures should be taken in cases of non-acceptance of election results, ie this article also needs to be supplemented.

Article 61 of the Law on General Elections in Kosovo which refers to the Mandate and Appointment of CEC Members should be completely depoliticized, practical cases have shown that CEC members are not independent from the influence of their parties and have left if they do not are obedient to party orders, Article 139 of the Constitution The CEC and its members after nomination by their parties call them independent but this is abused by the parties, giving the possibility of replacing them with a decision of political leaders, they have abused this right by removing them from the CEC.

The CEC with changes would be composed of judges and the academic world, so the CEC should have a mixed composition.

---

[52]Douche Welle , Kosovo: The final results of the elections are announced, Douqe Welle
  https://www.dw.com/sq/kosov%C3%AB-shpallen-rezultatet-p%C3%ABrfundimtare-t%C3%AB-
  zgjedhjeve/a-51153556,10.11.2020

The Law on General Elections of the Republic of Kosovo should change the role of the CEC, to be an oversight body of such mechanisms is: Municipal Election Commissions and Polling Station Councils.

The CEC has never been able to take full responsibility, although by law it must guarantee that there can be efficient access to polling stations around Kosovo, MECs and PSCs due to their political composition, not infrequently the CEC has not been able to obtain accurate information on what is happening at polling stations around Kosovo. Until now, the CEC, under Article 61 of the Law on General Elections, is the central body responsible for organizing and administering elections.

But electoral problems remain as follows: vote theft, or vote rigging by party commissions.

67.1 The Municipal Election Commission (MEC) shall generally consist of seven (7) members, this number may be increased if the number of political entities eligible to be part of the commission may

to be bigger.

MECs should be depoliticized and have a mixed composition of civil servants.

Article 74.1 deals with: the composition of Polling Station Councils (PSCs) that reflect the composition structure of members of political parties.

Some decision-making specifics of the MEC

The Municipal Election Commission, in special cases, may increase the number of members in the Polling Station Council and immediately notify the CEC.

The PSCs should be depoliticized because so far it has proven to be particularly harmful when counting the votes of individuals of political parties in the open proportional list, party commissioners in these councils have committed criminal offenses and some of them have been convicted by the courts.

So far, political party commissioners have been charged with many criminal offenses by the party members themselves who nominated them.

Article 110 of the Law on General Elections refers to the electoral system while Article 110.1 states that Kosovo is considered an area single electoral, after the amendment of the Law on General Elections, Kosovo should have 7 electoral zones based on the number of inhabitants. The depoliticized CEC would successfully implement adequate management of the electoral process.

5. The Challenge of Counting the Ballots by the Central Election Commission in Republic of Kosovo

One of the biggest challenges in the administration of elections in the Republic of Kosovo is the counting of votes after the end of election day[53]. One of the most chronic problems of the CEC[54] is the counting of votes of candidates of candidates of political parties in the electoral list. Counting is a challenge which affects the credibility of the elections and the fair administration of the vote of the party candidates.

The open proportional list as well as the commissioners of the political parties count the votes of their political parties and their candidates so far were a high challenge to achieve quality standards in the process of organizing elections and counting the votes and the final official publication by the Central Election Commission of Republic of Kosovo..

Counting the votes after election day in Kosovo is not a mathematical matter or simply counting the votes of political party candidates in parliamentary or local elections. The challenge is the same whether there will be an accurate vote count for party candidates, or party candidates filing their appeals to ECAP[55] and the Supreme Court?

5.1. Why should this process be shameful for party candidates?

The open list in the proportional[56] system helps party candidates to run for MP within the same party candidates. Candidates win individual votes from citizens within the open proportional list, candidates within the same party compete against each other, this has caused political problems within the same party, complaining against each other for votes stolen by their commissioners.

This causes major problems within a party by accusing each other or the political leader of directing the vote through party commissioners.

The accusations between the candidates of the same party are quite pronounced in the public opinion, the suspicions are that the commissioners of the political parties buy their votes from the commissioners of votes. Political party commissioners currently elect members of parliament, not citizens. Commissioners or members of the Polling Station Council, as defined by law at both levels, the law on parliamentary elections or

---

[53] See: After the elections, the vote counting process is a big problem and challenge for the CEC, due to the counting of the votes of the candidates by the commissioners of the political parties participating in the elections, the commissioners are often accused of stealing the votes of the party candidates. of them.

[54] See: Constitution of the Republic of Kosovo, Article 139 emphasizes the following: The Central Election Commission is a permanent body that prepares, supervises, directs and verifies all actions related to the election process and referendums and announces their results.

[55] Commission for Election Complaints and Appeals Panel (ECAP),Decisions, https://pzap.rks-gov.net/

[56] Kosovo practices the proportional system with open list.

the law on local elections, seem to be the biggest problem of election administration in the Republic of Kosovo.

Dissatisfaction is also associated with the party and suspicions that their votes have been stolen, this causes discord within the party and numerous accusations. and damage the public image of the CEC and the electorate.

The CEC is powerless to stop such a degrading process, as this electoral institution or electoral body also consists of the parliamentary parties of Kosovo, ie the parties that make up the CEC, this system of election administration by the political parties in Kosovo is presenting a big problem since 2000 when for the first time local elections were organized until October 6, 2019 to organize central or parliamentary elections or local election . So far there have been many recommendations to change the composition of Polling Station Councils but it has not happened until now. today in Kosovo. Numerous organizations have made their remarks and recommendations about the election administration process in Kosovo as follows: The Council of Europe[57], The European Union Election Observation Mission (EU EOM) through written reports.[58]

So far, political parties have not been willing to accept the depoliticization of the vote counting process, efforts have been lacking. The problem of vote depoliticization is quite challenging, there have been and will be remarks by international observers from the EU[59], the Council of Europe and many election observers in Kosovo as a result of the image deterioration. of elections that comes as a result of the counting of votes for party candidates. In Kosovo so far no party has taken seriously this issue, ie the removal of party commissioners in the counting of votes for candidates and political parties to replace them with servants civil.[60]

This is assessed in Kosovo as a lack of will to change the law for both local and general elections. The parties like this vote counting system and according to them it is more credible, and very few have dealt with the comments of many organizations about the negativity of the vote counting in the process. The political parties are not ready at all to make a reform of counting the votes, the CEC can only technically change the counting

---

[57] Council of Europe , Observation Mission KOSOVO V,CEEOM,5 October – 5 December 2007

[58] The European Union Election Observation Mission (EU EOM), KOSOVO1 LEGISLATIVE ELECTIONS 8 JUNE 2014, https://eeas.europa.eu/archives/eueom/missions/2014/kosovo/pdf/eu-eom-kosovo-2014-final-report_en.pdf,1.12.2020

[59] For more see the reports: The European Union Election Observation Mission (EU EOM) to Kosovo presented its Final Report on the 11 June 2017 legislative elections today. The report comprises an assessment of the electoral process and offers 26 recommendations to improve future electoral processes in Kosovo, 12.09.2017

[60] The civil service is composed of civil servants, impartial, professional, accountable and that highly reflects ethnicity and gender equality. Article 3.1 Of Civil servant Law.

of votes, ie to provide a faster result for the votes of the candidates, which is usually very late.

The counting process last lasted about two months. In the October 6 elections[61], an NISMA party claimed its votes had been stolen and caused a riot through complaints that delayed the certification of the final election results by almost three months. The NISMA party The Social Democrats had not crossed the preliminary election threshold.

The CEC carries out its activities through two laws:

- Law on General Elections
- Law on Local Elections
- Law on Political Parties
- Electoral Rules

These are the legal base of operation of CEC. All election operations are exercised on this legal basis.

The CEC may revise the technical rules from time to time, so it is competent to change these rules.

It is necessary to change some election rules. The issuance of a new regulation for the counting of votes is of great importance.

This is the competence of the CEC to do it and can serve it very positively in the faster counting of votes, especially of the candidates. The counting of votes from the diaspora is also of great importance to be done by the Center for Counting of Votes and Results (CRC)) as soon as possible and not as usual to leave them at the end after the counting of local votes. As it is known, Polling Station Councils in the polling stations do the counting of votes for both the parties and their candidates.

The Law on Elections deals with Polling Station Councils, composition, obligations, election of PSC members and other specifics. Based on the law, Polling Station Councils reflect the same structure of Municipal Election Boards (MECs). of those persons of who meet the relevant appointment criteria. The CECS (Article 74.4)[62] submits the list provided by the MEC to the CEC for approval, together with recommendations or remarks. The CEC reviews the list submitted by persons from the

---

[61] European Union Election Observation Mission KOSOVO 2019 Final Report. Report of 6 October 2019 . This Report contains to some extent the same recommendations as in previous reports. For more details see Report: http://www.epgencms.europarl.europa.eu/cmsdata/upload/1e4f1465-9cdd-4565-a837-a0487b092e51/Kosovo_early-legislative-elections_6-October-2019_final-report.pdf, 20.11.2020

[62] Law on General Elections, Article 74.4., https://gzk.rks-gov.net/ActDetail.aspx?ActID=2544.,4.12,2020

CEC Secretariat and decides with simple majority to appoint or not the persons presented, as the case may be.

Article 74.6 states the following: Any member of the PSC who does not participate in training organized by the MEC without good reason is prevented from working on Election Day and loses the right to part or all of the payment, as decided While Article 74.7[63] specifies what happens if a PSC member is absent on election day, this article specifies the following: Any PSC member who is not present at the polling station where he or she is scheduled to be on the day of Elections loses the right to payment and is immediately replaced by the MEC with a trained and appointed reserve member. Article 74.8[64] of the Law specifies the following: At the time of appointment, each PSC member signs the Code of Conduct, as provided by the CEC. All PSC members are obliged to implement the Code of Conduct during the work process.

Whereas Article 74.9[65] Every member of the PSC, regardless of the affiliation of a political party or political point of view, acts impartially in the service of all voters. This paragraph of this law is problematic and challenges the process and administration of elections in Kosovo since 2000[66] when for the first time in Kosovo were organized the first local elections under international administration, problems of this nature with the process of compliance with this paragraph CEC and MECs and PSCs faced challenging problems with criticism from local NGOs and international observers, the main problem remains the counting of the votes of their parties and their candidates, the main problem is the counting of individual votes of the candidates of their political parties. that the CEC receive major remarks as the main manager of the election administration in Kosovo from the candidates of political parties as well as from the international organizations that participate in the PSC observations on the day of the counting of the candidates' vote.

In order for the elections to have credibility, this problematic sub-issue must be changed, but here is a chain problem, if the composition of the PSC is changed, the composition of the MEC must be changed, and in the end the CEC, which is also composed of parties, must be depoliticized.

This issue remains absolutely difficult to change by political parties which must give up the administration of elections. This seems impossible in today's political circumstances in Kosovo, until the change of this article and this chain of responsibility Kosovo will have difficult to pass the election process without problems, without penalties of the commissioners of political parties and finally to be given a positive note by the Council

---

[63] Law on General Elections, Article 74.6, https://gzk.rks-gov.net/ActDetail.aspx?ActID=2544.,2.12,2020
[64] Law on General Elections, Article 74.8 https://gzk.rks-gov.net/ActDetail.aspx?ActID=2544.,2.12,2020
[65] Law on General Elections, Article 74.9 https://gzk.rks-gov.net/ActDetail.aspx?ActID=2544.,2.12,2020
[66] First local election organize from UNMIK/UN Administration in Kosovo

of Europe and the EU which regularly participate in election observation. The demands of the EC and the EU were numerous in this regard, they demanded and still require an electoral reform. In Kosovo, in my opinion, the electoral system should be reformed, which should be changed to a semi-majority system by establishing constituencies. But this is being hindered from political parties which are not at all interested in taking more areas and the representation of citizens to be from many areas and not only from one constituency, to remind that Kosovo is an electoral zone. So, the problems with the electoral system originate from political parties and not by citizens.

If the citizens were asked, Kosovo would have to consist of several areas.

5.2. Why more constituencies?

The answer is simple because political parties would be obliged to have candidates from certain areas and not like until now where the representation is not correct in the Assembly of Kosovo, where political parties bypass large constituencies and run their own people according to their will free but not mandatory. Let us remind you that women would also have problems running

for elections if the law does not oblige political parties to run 30% of their electoral list for any level of elections, whether parliamentary or local. So, the law is very clear and precise political parties are obliged to run 30% of women on their competing list. Considering that the CEC is the main manager and responsible for the organization of elections, Article 76.1 states the following: Each PSC is approved by the CEC and headed by the Chairman. Article 76.3 [67]The CECS requires new political entities, NGOs and organizations other citizens to submit additional nominations for PSC. Article 76.4[68] states as follows: All nominations under section 74.2[69] and 74.3[70] of this law shall be submitted to the respective MEC no later than five (5) days after the nomination request has been made by the CEC Secretariat.

While Article 76.5[71] speaks for the List of PSC nominations that should include the following:

a) the name of the political entity or NGO that made the request, the name of the contact person and the details

his / her contact;

b) name, surname, personal number, date of birth of each appointee;

---

[67] Law on General Elections, Article 76.3,   https://gzk.rks-gov.net/ActDetail.aspx?ActID=2544.,8.12,2020
[68] Law on General Elections, Article 76.4,   https://gzk.rks-gov.net/ActDetail.aspx?ActID=2544.,2.12,2020
[69] Law on General Elections, Article 74.2,   https://gzk.rks-gov.net/ActDetail.aspx?ActID=2544.,2.12,2020
[70] Law on General Elections, Article 74.3,   https://gzk.rks-gov.net/ActDetail.aspx?ActID=2544.,2.12,2020
[71] Law on General Elections, Article 76.5 https://gzk.rks-gov.net/ActDetail.aspx?ActID=2544.,8.12,2020

c) a detailed description of each nominee if he / she has previous election experience and

high school diploma; and

d) date and place of submission of the list of nominations, signature of the representative of the political entity or the NGO, as well as the signing of the acceptance of the list by the MEC representative.

Article 77.1[72] states as follows: Immediately upon receipt of all nominations, the MECs appoint the nominees to the PSs.

proposed to them by applying the following set of rules: a) no more than one person from a list of PSC nominations, submitted under Article 76.2[73] to be appointed a PSC member in the same PS (Polling Station);

b) during the selection of candidates from the list of PSC nominations submitted under Article 76.3[74], priority shall be given to candidates of the best quality and especially to those with previous experience in election, this paragraph has never been implemented by political parties that have nominated their members, they have nominated their loyalists but not people more prepared and capable of the process.

c) no more than one close family member may be appointed to the same PSC. For the purposes of this article, close family includes spouse, children, parents and siblings;

d) in new municipalities or where the results from previous elections have not been certified, the membership of PSCs is selected by lot among those political entities certified to participate in the elections of future in that municipality.

The Electoral Rule also speaks for the PSC Article 4 of this rule The PSC is said to be led by the PSC Chairman specifying that the other members of the MA are as follows: Voter Line Controller, Voter Identification Officer, Ballot Issuer and Ballot Box Supervisor.

The Electoral Rule [75]also speaks for the PSC Article 4 of this rule The PSC is said to be led by the PSC Chairman specifying that the other members of the MA are as follows:

Voter Line Controller, Voter Identification Officer, Ballot Issuer and Ballot Box Supervisor. Article 5[76] of this election rule specifies as follows who may not be a PSC

---

[72] Law on General Elections, Article 77.1 https://gzk.rks-gov.net/ActDetail.aspx?ActID=2544.,2.12,2020
[73] Law on General Elections, Article 76.2, https://gzk.rks-gov.net/ActDetail.aspx?ActID=2544.,2.12,2020
[74] Law on General Elections, Article 76.3, https://gzk.rks-gov.net/ActDetail.aspx?ActID=2544.,2.12,2020
[75] Election Regulation No. 09/2013 – Voting, Counting in Polling Station and Management of Polling Center, https://www.kqz-ks.org/an/rregullat-zgjedhore/,7.12.2020

member as follows: Candidate for office elected in Kosovo, Member of any assembly in Kosovo and abroad, Member of any MEC, CECS, CEC, member of the police, or member of the Kosovo Security Force, or of any military service, declared mentally incompetent by decision of any court, has been found guilty of a criminal offense during the last three years by a final court decision, is prohibited by the ECAP decision to be an administrative part of an electoral body, has been found guilty of a criminal offense during the last three years by a final decision that cut by the court.

6.The Challenge of Counting the Ballots by the Central Election Commission in Republic of Kosovo

One of the biggest challenges in the administration of elections in the Republic of Kosovo is the counting of votes after the end of election day[77]. One of the most chronic problems of the CEC[78] is the counting of votes of candidates of candidates of political parties in the electoral list. Counting is a challenge which affects the credibility of the elections and the fair administration of the vote of the party candidates.

The open proportional list as well as the commissioners of the political parties count the votes of their political parties and their candidates so far were a high challenge to achieve quality standards in the process of organizing elections and counting the votes and the final official publication by the Central Election Commission of Republic of Kosovo.

Counting the votes after election day in Kosovo is not a mathematical matter or simply counting the votes of political party candidates in parliamentary or local elections. The challenge is the same whether there will be an accurate vote count for party candidates, or party candidates filing their appeals to ECAP[79] and the Supreme Court?

6.1.Why should this process be shameful for party candidates?

---

[76] Election Regulation No. 09/2013 – Voting, Counting in Polling Station and Management of Polling Center, Article 5, https://www.kqz-ks.org/an/rregullat-zgjedhore/,6.12.2020

[77] See: After the elections, the vote counting process is a big problem and challenge for the CEC, due to the counting of the votes of the candidates by the commissioners of the political parties participating in the elections, the commissioners are often accused of stealing the votes of the party candidates. of them.

[78] See: Constitution of the Republic of Kosovo, Article 139 emphasizes the following: The Central Election Commission is a permanent body that prepares, supervises, directs and verifies all actions related to the election process and referendums and announces their results.

[79] Commission for Election Complaints and Appeals Panel (ECAP),Decisions, https://pzap.rks-gov.net/

The open list in the proportional[80] system helps party candidates to run for MP within the same party candidates. Candidates win individual votes from citizens within the open proportional list, candidates within the same party compete against each other, this has caused political problems within the same party, complaining against each other for votes stolen by their commissioners.

This causes major problems within a party by accusing each other or the political leader of directing the vote through party commissioners.

The accusations between the candidates of the same party are quite pronounced in the public opinion, the suspicions are that the commissioners of the political parties buy their votes from the commissioners of votes. Political party commissioners currently elect members of parliament, not citizens. Commissioners or members of the Polling Station Council, as defined by law at both levels, the law on parliamentary elections or the law on local elections, seem to be the biggest problem of election administration in the Republic of Kosovo.

Dissatisfaction is also associated with the party and suspicions that their votes have been stolen, this causes discord within the party and numerous accusations. and damage the public image of the CEC and the electorate.

The CEC is powerless to stop such a degrading process, as this electoral institution or electoral body also consists of the parliamentary parties of Kosovo, ie the parties that make up the CEC, this system of election administration by the political parties in Kosovo is presenting a big problem since 2000 when for the first time local elections were organized until October 6, 2019 to organize central or parliamentary elections or local election . So far there have been many recommendations to change the composition of Polling Station Councils but it has not happened until now. today in Kosovo. Numerous organizations have made their remarks and recommendations about the election administration process in Kosovo as follows: The Council of Europe[81], The European Union Election Observation Mission (EU EOM) through written reports.[82]

So far, political parties have not been willing to accept the depoliticization of the vote counting process, efforts have been lacking. The problem of vote depoliticization is quite challenging, there have been and will be remarks by international observers from the

---

[80] Kosovo practices the proportional system with open list.

[81] Council of Europe , Observation Mission KOSOVO V,CEEOM,5 October – 5 December 2007

[82] The European Union Election Observation Mission (EU EOM), KOSOVO1 LEGISLATIVE ELECTIONS 8 JUNE 2014, https://eeas.europa.eu/archives/eueom/missions/2014/kosovo/pdf/eu-eom-kosovo-2014-final-report_en.pdf,1.12.2020

EU[83], the Council of Europe and many election observers in Kosovo as a result of the image deterioration. of elections that comes as a result of the counting of votes for party candidates. In Kosovo so far no party has taken seriously this issue, ie the removal of party commissioners in the counting of votes for candidates and political parties to replace them with servants civil.[84]

This is assessed in Kosovo as a lack of will to change the law for both local and general elections. The parties like this vote counting system and according to them it is more credible, and very few have dealt with the comments of many organizations about the negativity of the vote counting in the process. The political parties are not ready at all to make a reform of counting the votes, the CEC can only technically change the counting of votes, ie to provide a faster result for the votes of the candidates, which is usually very late.

The counting process last lasted about two months. In the October 6 elections[85], an NISMA party claimed its votes had been stolen and caused a riot through complaints that delayed the certification of the final election results by almost three months. The NISMA party The Social Democrats had not crossed the preliminary election threshold.

The CEC carries out its activities through two laws:

- Law on General Elections
- Law on Local Elections
- Law on Political Parties
- Electoral Rules

These are the legal base of operation of CEC. All election operations are exercised on this legal basis.

The CEC may revise the technical rules from time to time, so it is competent to change these rules.

It is necessary to change some election rules. The issuance of a new regulation for the counting of votes is of great importance.

---

[83] For more see the reports: The European Union Election Observation Mission (EU EOM) to Kosovo presented its Final Report on the 11 June 2017 legislative elections today. The report comprises an assessment of the electoral process and offers 26 recommendations to improve future electoral processes in Kosovo, 12.09.2017

[84] The civil service is composed of civil servants, impartial, professional, accountable and that highly reflects ethnicity and gender equality. Article 3.1 Of Civil servant Law.

[85] European Union Election Observation Mission KOSOVO 2019 Final Report. Report of 6 October 2019 . This Report contains to some extent the same recommendations as in previous reports. For more details see Report: http://www.epgencms.europarl.europa.eu/cmsdata/upload/1e4f1465-9cdd-4565-a837-a0487b092e51/Kosovo_early-legislative-elections_6-October-2019_final-report.pdf, 20.11.2020

This is the competence of the CEC to do it and can serve it very positively in the faster counting of votes, especially of the candidates. The counting of votes from the diaspora is also of great importance to be done by the Center for Counting of Votes and Results (CRC)) as soon as possible and not as usual to leave them at the end after the counting of local votes. As it is known,   Polling Station Councils in the polling stations do the counting of votes for both the parties and their candidates.

The Law on Elections deals with Polling Station Councils, composition, obligations, election of PSC members and other specifics. Based on the law, Polling Station Councils reflect the same structure of Municipal Election Boards (MECs). of those persons of who meet the relevant appointment criteria. The CECS (Article 74.4)[86] submits the list provided by the MEC to the CEC for approval, together with recommendations or remarks. The CEC reviews the list submitted by persons from the CEC Secretariat and decides with simple majority to appoint or not the persons presented, as the case may be.

Article 74.6 states the following: Any member of the PSC who does not participate in training organized by the MEC without good reason is prevented from working on Election Day and loses the right to part or all of the payment, as decided While Article 74.7[87] specifies what happens if a PSC member is absent on election day, this article specifies the following: Any PSC member who is not present at the polling station where he or she is scheduled to be on the day of Elections loses the right to payment and is immediately replaced by the MEC with a trained and appointed reserve member. Article 74.8[88] of the Law specifies the following: At the time of appointment, each PSC member signs the Code of Conduct, as provided by the CEC. All PSC members are obliged to implement the Code of Conduct during the work process.

Whereas Article 74.9[89] Every member of the PSC, regardless of the affiliation of a political party or political point of view, acts impartially in the service of all voters. This paragraph of this law is problematic and challenges the process and administration of elections in Kosovo since 2000[90] when for the first time in Kosovo were organized the first local elections under international administration, problems of this nature with the process of compliance with this paragraph CEC and MECs and PSCs faced challenging problems with criticism from local NGOs and international observers, the main problem remains the counting of the votes of their parties and their candidates, the main problem is the counting of individual votes of the candidates of their political parties. that the CEC receive major remarks as the main manager of the election administration in

---

[86] Law on General Elections, Article 74.4., https://gzk.rks-gov.net/ActDetail.aspx?ActID=2544.,4.12,2020
[87] Law on General Elections, Article 74.6, https://gzk.rks-gov.net/ActDetail.aspx?ActID=2544.,2.12,2020
[88] Law on General Elections, Article 74.8 https://gzk.rks-gov.net/ActDetail.aspx?ActID=2544.,2.12,2020
[89] Law on General Elections, Article 74.9 https://gzk.rks-gov.net/ActDetail.aspx?ActID=2544.,2.12,2020
[90] First local election organize from UNMIK/UN Administration in Kosovo

Kosovo from the candidates of political parties as well as from the international organizations that participate in the PSC observations on the day of the counting of the candidates' vote.

In order for the elections to have credibility, this problematic sub-issue must be changed, but here is a chain problem, if the composition of the PSC is changed, the composition of the MEC must be changed, and in the end the CEC, which is also composed of parties, must be depoliticized.

This issue remains absolutely difficult to change by political parties which must give up the administration of elections. This seems impossible in today's political circumstances in Kosovo, until the change of this article and this chain of responsibility Kosovo will have difficult to pass the election process without problems, without penalties of the commissioners of political parties and finally to be given a positive note by the Council of Europe and the EU which regularly participate in election observation. The demands of the EC and the EU were numerous in this regard, they demanded and still require an electoral reform. In Kosovo, in my opinion, the electoral system should be reformed, which should be changed to a semi-majority system by establishing constituencies. But this is being hindered from political parties which are not at all interested in taking more areas and the representation of citizens to be from many areas and not only from one constituency, to remind that Kosovo is an electoral zone. So, the problems with the electoral system originate from political parties and not by citizens.

If the citizens were asked, Kosovo would have to consist of several areas.

6.2. Political Parties Candidates ?

The answer is simple because political parties would be obliged to have candidates from certain areas and not like until now where the representation is not correct in the Assembly of Kosovo, where political parties bypass large constituencies and run their own people according to their will free but not mandatory. Let us remind you that women would also have problems running

for elections if the law does not oblige political parties to run 30% of their electoral list for any level of elections, whether parliamentary or local. So, the law is very clear and precise political parties are obliged to run 30% of women on their competing list. Considering that the CEC is the main manager and responsible for the organization of elections, Article 76.1 states the following: Each PSC is approved by the CEC and headed by the Chairman. Article 76.3 [91]The CECS requires new political entities, NGOs and organizations other citizens to submit additional nominations for PSC. Article 76.4[92]

---

[91] Law on General Elections, Article 76.3,   https://gzk.rks-gov.net/ActDetail.aspx?ActID=2544.,8.12,2020
[92] Law on General Elections, Article 76.4,   https://gzk.rks-gov.net/ActDetail.aspx?ActID=2544.,2.12,2020

states as follows: All nominations under section 74.2[93] and 74.3[94] of this law shall be submitted to the respective MEC no later than five (5) days after the nomination request has been made by the CEC Secretariat.

While Article 76.5[95] speaks for the List of PSC nominations that should include the following:

a) the name of the political entity or NGO that made the request, the name of the contact person and the detailshis / her contact;

b) name, surname, personal number, date of birth of each appointee;

c) a detailed description of each nominee if he / she has previous election experience and high school diploma; and

d) date and place of submission of the list of nominations, signature of the representative of the political entity or the NGO, as well as the signing of the acceptance of the list by the MEC representative.

Article 77.1[96] states as follows: Immediately upon receipt of all nominations, the MECs appoint the nominees to the PSs.

proposed to them by applying the following set of rules: a) no more than one person from a list of PSC nominations, submitted under Article 76.2[97] to be appointed a PSC member in the same PS (Polling Station);

b) during the selection of candidates from the list of PSC nominations submitted under Article 76.3[98], priority shall be given to candidates of the best quality and especially to those with previous experience in election, this paragraph has never been implemented by political parties that have nominated their members, they have nominated their loyalists but not people more prepared and capable of the process.

c) no more than one close family member may be appointed to the same PSC. For the purposes of this article, close family includes spouse, children, parents and siblings;

d) in new municipalities or where the results from previous elections have not been certified, the membership of PSCs is selected by lot among those political entities certified to participate in the elections of future in that municipality.

---

[93] Law on General Elections, Article 74.2, https://gzk.rks-gov.net/ActDetail.aspx?ActID=2544.,2.12,2020
[94] Law on General Elections, Article 74.3, https://gzk.rks-gov.net/ActDetail.aspx?ActID=2544.,2.12,2020
[95] Law on General Elections, Article 76.5 https://gzk.rks-gov.net/ActDetail.aspx?ActID=2544.,8.12,2020
[96] Law on General Elections, Article 77.1 https://gzk.rks-gov.net/ActDetail.aspx?ActID=2544.,2.12,2020
[97] Law on General Elections, Article 76.2, https://gzk.rks-gov.net/ActDetail.aspx?ActID=2544.,2.12,2020
[98] Law on General Elections, Article 76.3, https://gzk.rks-gov.net/ActDetail.aspx?ActID=2544.,2.12,2020

The Electoral Rule also speaks for the PSC Article 4 of this rule The PSC is said to be led by the PSC Chairman specifying that the other members of the MA are as follows: Voter Line Controller, Voter Identification Officer, Ballot Issuer and Ballot Box Supervisor.

The Electoral Rule [99]also speaks for the PSC Article 4 of this rule The PSC is said to be led by the PSC Chairman specifying that the other members of the MA are as follows:

Voter Line Controller, Voter Identification Officer, Ballot Issuer and Ballot Box Supervisor. Article 5[100] of this election rule specifies as follows who may not be a PSC member as follows: Candidate for office elected in Kosovo, Member of any assembly in Kosovo and abroad, Member of any MEC, CECS, CEC, member of the police, or member of the Kosovo Security Force, or of any military service, declared mentally incompetent by decision of any court, has been found guilty of a criminal offense during the last three years by a final court decision, is prohibited by the ECAP decision to be an administrative part of an electoral body, has been found guilty of a criminal offense during the last three years by a final decision that cut by the court.

6.3. Political Development in Kosovo

The elections in Kosovo are a result of the political situation created in Kosovo after the Prime Minister's resignation, the reasons for the resignation were not due to an invitation sent by Prime Minister Haradinaj but the resignation was due to the US and EU requesting to abolish taxes on Serbian goods, and this had not been accepted by Haradinaj, which led to the extraordinary elections in Kosovo. Haradinaj had also made a platform for dialogue with Serbia that was not taken seriously neither in Kosovo nor in Brussels, a document that was more work-related to what should be dealt with in the Kosovo-Serbia negotiations and without detail. A law was later drafted for dialogue which was rejected by the Constitutional Court which decision addressed powers to negotiate to the Government and did not go large, PDK aware that Thaci will be deprived of the right to represent Kosovo in negotiations with Serbia, has been forced the government of state to resign. The elections were organized without prior reform of the election law, all issues remain the same. Kosovo needs reform in two respects:
Legal and technical, so these two reforms should happen as soon as possible, but that did not happen, the elections were organized by the current law and with the same trouble. The voter list was not cleared from dead citizen, which remains the biggest concern.
- The conditional vote should be abolished
- Municipal Election Commissions should be depoliticized
- Polling stations should be depoliticized

---

[99] Election Regulation No. 09/2013 – Voting, Counting in Polling Station and Management of Polling Center, https://www.kqz-ks.org/an/rregullat-zgjedhore/,7.12.2020
[100] Election Regulation No. 09/2013 – Voting, Counting in Polling Station and Management of Polling Center, Article 5, https://www.kqz-ks.org/an/rregullat-zgjedhore/,6.12.2020

- Central Election Commission should also be fully depoliticized
- Division of electoral zone should be done soon is possible.
- A new law should be issued for the political party
- Political parties must be registered in the courts
- Political parties working in contravention of the state constitution should be removed from the political activity register
- All votes must be counted at polling stations and only diaspora votes will have to be counted at the Ballot Counting Center.
- The law on transparency of political party donations should be issued by Parliament of Kosovo
- 40,000.00 thousand invalid votes in October 2019 by-elections

- 45% of citizens have voted in the October 2019 snap elections

- Political parties compline: ECAP decision-making regarding complaints of political entities and candidates for MPs after the announcement of the final results of the elections of 06 October 2019The Election Complaints and Appeals Panel - ECAP, announces public opinion that, by 10:50 today, has decided on all appeals filed by political entities and candidates for deputies that have been filed after the results of the election have been announced and final. by the Central Election Commission - CEC, on 07.11.2019[101].
  ECAP has once started notifying parties with decisions on their   grievances.

The Complaints Panel has decided as follows:

The ECAP received 53 complaints based on them in relation to 52 complaints the panel decided to order the CEC to recount 1472 polling stations. While regarding the complaint lodged by the Initiative - AKR - DP Coalition, it has decided to accept the complaint as grounded and has ordered the CEC to remove from the final election result the votes of the voters outside Kosovo who came from Serbia[102].First from this administrative organ was asked to recount 430 polling stations.

23 complaints were dismissed as untimely and inadmissible[103].

25 complaints were rejected as ungrounded[104].

1 complaint is found to be withdrawn[105].

---

[101] PZAP,http://pzap.rks-gov.net/?p=9752,23.11.2019

[102] PZAP,http://pzap.rks-gov.net/?p=9752,23.11.2019

[103] PZAP,http://pzap.rks-gov.net/?p=9752,23.11.2019

[104] PZAP,http://pzap.rks-gov.net/?p=9752,23.11.2019

6.4. Coalition possibility

The LDK and VV coalition impossible, there are many reasons to fail, first of all the completely different program, the commitments for the state of Kosovo are different, VV failed to recognize the developments in Kosovo, there are also many Kosovar politicians who did not favor this anarchic party.

Coalition possibilities	
VV LDK	Remarks : • Complication until reaching agreement? • Expert of two political party work on the details. • Government should have around 12 Ministries • Governance program will be drafted

The LDK is a right-wing party seeking privatization of publicly owned enterprises while VV wants to hold the post as a public asset. VV wants to establish Commercial Bank with people's money, LDK does not support the concept of a state-owned bank, what is common may be the Economic Development Fund.[106]
Protecting workers at work, strengthening the labor inspectorate, fining private companies if they do not respect the employment contract, strengthening public funds, paying regular pension contributions every month. Highly needed health protection for all citizens, the law has long been approved by the Assembly and so far no implementation has taken place in the absence of political knowledge and will. State education reform is also an important topic as VV opposes the private education sector as the dominant area of education in Kosovo and requires it to be reformed just as the Public Universities need to be reformed. The development of vocational schools is important to mention by the two main political parties in the state of Kosovo. These two political parties have completely different programs and commitments, the VV program in Kosovo is explained as impossible for a market economy, the VV reform is completely necessary, this party has no proper political framework, and the VV victory is only minimal. 1%, so this does not give this party convenience but should be completely flexible, remarks in the political vocabulary of this party have the other party LDK which

---

105 PZAP,http://pzap.rks-gov.net/?p=9752,23.11.2019
106 PZAP,http://pzap.rks-gov.net/?p=9752,23.11.2019

is the second party to vote in Kosovo in the October 6, 2019 elections. The biggest difference between these two political parties is the issue of dialogue with Serbia on normalizing relations, the VV is in no hurry to engage in dialogue, and requires review of all Kosovo-Serbia agreements so far, while the LDK fully recognize the agreements reached so far, although some of them may be revised, the LDK requires the implementation of these agreements, including the agreement on the association of Serb municipalities based on the decision of Constitutional Court- ruling referring to this association, which may not have executive powers this association. VV has an unbalanced political vocabulary for many developments both in the region and in Kosovo, public administration reform is needed and is an EU requirement, VV thinks that DE politicization should take place, but it is not the only deep - politicization problem, the problem remains great employment beyond requirements and needs. U.S. support to Kosovo and Serbia in the Dialogue process requires teamwork: Special Presidential Envoy Grenell and State Department Special Representative Matt Palmer together in Berlin. Both will visit Kosovo. Grenel was very clear should be an final agreement Kosovo-Serbia with 3 or 4 month, VV is very skeptic and asked not to be hurry in this process and not to precise month for achieving agreement. In the public opinion, such a coalition is almost impossible, given the great differences, it is thought that these parties cannot develop the state with these contradictions between them. working alongside a coalition, LDK fears VV may run until term ends. The issue of vetting and enforcement in the judiciary is an issue that is well-settled by both parties, the law on vetting is required, while enforcement must be carried out by an independent body of independent professionals, with EU support and support. The problem is complicated and may be hampered by the justice system. VV has stated that it will not form a coalition with PDK, AAK and NISMA, which are considered corrupt parties by the people, which complicates the agreement for a joint government with these parties. If LDK refuses to join coalition with VV then VV will ask again to go to the new election. VV has also stated that it will not go into coalition with the Serbian list manipulated by Serbia.

VV– decision	VV rules: not passible co-governance in coalition with PDK, AAK, NISMA and Serbian List
	Will be new election if failed coalition with LDK

6.5. Political campaign for 6 October election in Kosovo

Pre-election campaign started a month before the elections day, this campaign is illegal by the law on elections in force, however all private television stations in Kosovo have invited parties to present their program opinions, even though the pre-election campaigns were illegal. They were made but ECAP as a body and CEC did not react in front of the fields, for every night there was also some kind of electronic voting online, every citizen who voted electronically on these televisions means breaking the electoral acts in force. The Election Commission is made up of political parties; therefore it was never dictated to this institution to stop this party pre-election. Independent but the members of this institution are nominated by political leaders. The political parties in Kosovo control and count their votes, this is very problematic for neutral work, the biggest problem is the counting of candidate votes for deputies, in this situation each political party counts the votes of its candidates and in these situations there are always abuses.

Pre-election campaign
Remarks: Campaign is illegal by the law on elections in force

Leaders of the two parties that did best in the weekend Kosovo elections have both signaled their interest in forming a coalition government.

The two former opposition parties that won most votes in Kosovo's recent parliamentary elections have expressed willingness to reach a coalition agreement, four days after the voters elected a new parliament.

After Albin Kurti's Vetevendosje party came first in last Sunday's vote, the Democratic League of Kosovo's candidate for prime minister, Vjosa Osmani, on Wednesday on Facebook called for a coalition agreement between them,but as well this party always have some reasons to live negotiation.

"Finally, citizens not only voted but through their votes, called for changes and the punishment of bad governance, this kind of conclusion come from public opinion" LDK declared . "Citizens also decided for the new government that should be composed of the opposition parties [the LDK and Vetevendosje]," but is really which is going to happened? Citizen they want to see changes as well International Community.

"To me, there is no other alternative left . An LDK-VV coalition has many challenges ahead of it, but it should have only one interest: that of Kosovo's citizens which wants something to change,"

With all the votes apart from postal ballots counted, the Vetevendosje (Self-Determination) party was in the lead after polling 203,052 votes, or 25.49 per cent of the votes cast. It was just ahead of the LDK, which polled 197,702 votes[107], or 24.82[108] per cent of the votes cast.

Kadri Veseli's former ruling Democratic Party of Kosovo, PDK, came in third place, winning only 169,211[109] votes, or 21.24[110] per cent of the votes cast.

Outgoing Prime Minister Ramush Haradinaj's coalition between his Alliance for the Future of Kosovo, AAK and the Social Democrats came fourth with 92,149 votes, or

---

[107] CEC,https://www.kqz-ks.org/zgjedhjet-e-pergjithshme/zgjedhjet-per-kuvend-te-kosoves-2019/

[108] CEC, https://www.kqz-ks.org/zgjedhjet-e-pergjithshme/zgjedhjet-per-kuvend-te-kosoves-2019/

[109] CEC, https://www.kqz-ks.org/zgjedhjet-e-pergjithshme/zgjedhjet-per-kuvend-te-kosoves-2019/

[110] CEC ,https://www.kqz-ks.org/zgjedhjet-e-pergjithshme/zgjedhjet-per-kuvend-te-kosoves-2019/

11.57 per cent of the votes cast. AAK and PSD was very hoped to have around 18% , this time did not happened

On Tuesday night, Vetevendosje's prime ministerial candidate, Kurti, echoed Vjosa Osmani's words, saying that there was "no other option" to a coalition with the LDK. "We cannot substitute the LDK with the PDK, AAK and NISMA," he said, referring to the other parties.It going to happened how will look such a coalition if we talk about performance.

"I will start negotiations with the LDK based on the election result and finally agree. If we cannot find an agreement, we will go to new elections," Kurti told Pristina-based on KTV with enthusiasm to not forget the wish is something and reality something else .

The final composition of the new parliament remains unclear after a coalition formed between two outgoing deputy prime ministers, Fatmir Limaj and his NISMA party and Behgjet Pacolli of the New Kosovo Alliance, AKR, polled below the threshold of 4 per cent of votes cast, at 4.96 [111]per cent, according to public opinion its good because of destructive role of NISMA in education which was leaded 2017-2019.

The NISMA-AKR coalition's hopes of passing the threshold now rest on uncounted postal ballots, coming mainly from Kosovo's large diaspora.

6.6. Before election and expected opposition

The opposition had hoped to win an absolute majority in the by-elections, although the former opposition was split, with each of the former opposition parties running alone in the new -elections. The public opinion wanted to be in a pre-election coalition LDK -VV, it did not happen, the main problem was who is going to have the Prime Minister, and the political paths were divided. Citizens' enthusiasm subsided when the two parties decided to run alone, the majority reacted negatively and despaired. LDK and VV in these elections were seen as a new hope for Kosovo to fight organized crime and corruption, enrich politicians illegally.

6.7.Kosovo election: Opposition parties claim win

Ex-Opposition parties have claimed the greatest number of votes in Kosovo's general election.

Centre-left Vetevendosje and Centre-Right Democratic League (LDK) are each expected to win about 25% of the vote. [112]

The election was called in July when Prime Minister Ramush Haradinaj resigned to face questioning by a war crimes court in The Hague.Nobody believe in Kosovo reasons of PM resignation, Haradinaj was motivated from some people in AAK that is better to

---

[111] CEC ,https://www.kqz-ks.org/zgjedhjet-e-pergjithshme/zgjedhjet-per-kuvend-te-kosoves-2019/

[112] CEC, https://www.kqz-ks.org/zgjedhjet-e-pergjithshme/zgjedhjet-per-kuvend-te-kosoves-2019/

resign and maybe could have great result in new election, the reason of resignation was problem of tax for Serbia.

It is the fourth election since Kosovo declared independence from Serbia in 2008.

Serbia does not recognize State of Kosovo and with Russia has blocked it from becoming a member of the UN and other international bodies.

- War crimes claims against PM hang over Kosovo vote
- Kosovo hits Serbia with 100% trade tariffs

In talks before the vote, Vetevendosje and the LDK failed to agree on forming a coalition.

Both parties promise to tackle unemployment and fight crime and corruption.

Vetevendosje's leader Albin Kurti said he would "knock on the LDK door" on Monday to start negotiations.

6.8.Can the biggest parties work together?

There are opinions that these two political party LDK and VV do not have nothing in common, but the general demand of the citizens is that these two parties join the coalition for their own good, although hopes are low to see any change. By and large, most of the programmatic points are at odds with Kosovo's market economy and constitution.

The two parties celebrating the most are very different in character

Vetevendosje is an anti-establishment Albanian nationalist movement. Its MPs are notorious for disrupting sessions of the National Assembly by lobbing tear gas[113]. The LDK is Kosovo's oldest party - and hopes to install lawyer Vjosa Osmani as the first female prime minister[114].

The two parties failed to reach a coalition agreement before the election - and may take many weeks or month of negotiations to form a new government the risk is to not happened ever this coalition. And can occur difficult situations or can be more complications in future, or may we have a new election?

Meanwhile, the former leaders of the Kosovo Liberation Army are licking their electoral wounds. Voters held their parties largely responsible for endemic corruption and a lack of development.

---

[113] **De Launey, Balkans Correspondent/BBC, October 2019**
[114] **De Launey, Balkans Correspondent/BBC, October 2019**

Mr Haradinaj's party meanwhile is set to win only 11.5 % of the vote.[115]

The 51-year-old served as commander in the 1998-1999 Kosovo conflict, which eventually led to Kosovo declaring independence in 2008.

Mr Haradinaj stepped down so that he could attend court as an ordinary citizen - but was free to stand for re-election because no indictments have yet been announced.

He denies war crimes and has been tried and acquitted twice before at the UN tribunal[116].

Image copyright EPA Image caption The LDK hopes Vjosa Osmani will become Kosovo's first female prime minister in future/

Last November, he imposed a 100% tariff on imports from Serbia in retaliation for Belgrade blocking Kosovo's membership of international organizations.

- The town where neighbors won't share a coffee
- Land swap could bridge divide for Serbia and Kosovo

He has ignored pleas from Brussels to revoke the tariffs.

Mr Kurti has said his party will abolish the tariffs but will introduce other retaliatory measures against Serbia.

Meanwhile Serbia's President Aleksandar Vucic says Belgrade will hold talks with the Kosovan government once the tariffs have been removed.

 US President Donald Trump appointed the US ambassador to Germany, Richard Grenell, as special envoy for peace negotiations between Kosovo and Serbia. Until now Kosovo was recognize from 116 international stats.

Kosovo is recognized by most of the west state but it needs Belgrade, Russia and China to accept its statehood to get a seat in the United Nations.

7. Opposition parties overturn Kosovo politics with election victory/euronews[117]

The opposition leftist Vetevendosje (Self- determination) party looked set to come first in Kosovo's parliamentary poll, but it will have to negotiate a coalition to form a government with other political parties. It will not be easy to find a political partners to start a governance in Kosovo , because the proportional system its make a lot a trouble and reflect very negative concerning to established government in Kosovo[118].The

[115] CEC,https://www.kqz-ks.org/zgjedhjet-e-pergjithshme/zgjedhjet-per-kuvend-te-kosoves-2019/
[116] **De Launey, Balkans Correspondent/BBC,October2019**
[117] Euonews: Opposition parties overturn Kosovo politics with election victory,October, 2019
[118] Euonews: Opposition parties overturn Kosovo politics with election victory,October, 2019

result was very tide between two ex -opposition party in Kosovo. Not much hope about future cooperation of this two political party LDK and VV?

Preliminary results showed it had won 26% of votes with 82% of ballots counted, while another opposition party — the centre-right Democratic League of Kosovo (LDK) — won 25% of votes.

7.1. Supporters celebrated in Pristina on Sunday evening

The early election happened after Prime Minister Ramush Harra-din-aj resigned ahead of questioning in the Hague by an investigation into war crimes in Serbia two decades ago.

The Democratic Party of Kosovo (PDK) was third with 21% while a list headed by the outgoing Prime Minister, Ramush Haradinaj, got 11.5% of votes.

It signals a new era for politics in the Balkan nation, whose leadership was previously dominated by figureheads from the country's late-1990s ethnic conflict and war of independence[119].

Kosovars will cast their ballots on Sunday, October 6, to pick a new parliament in snap elections.

Rampant corruption, widespread unemployment and sour relations with neighboring Serbia are themes dominating the poll — and must be addressed if the country is to make progress toward EU membership[120].

The election was triggered when Prime Minister Ramush Haradinaj resigned after a war crimes court in The Hague summoned him for questioning as a suspect. It concerned his role in the 1998-99 insurgencies against Serb forces.

Here's what you need to know about the elections.

7.2. Kosovo and Serbia: still at odds

Predominantly Albanian Kosovo declared its independence in February 2008, when Serbia rejected the declaration as illegal but Europe's major powers and the United States recognized the move.

Where do things stand 20 years since the former Yugoslav territories were at the center of one of Europe's most violent conflicts? In short, Serbia considers Kosovo part of its territory but Kosovo considers itself an independent state.

---

[119] Euonews: Opposition parties overturn Kosovo politics with election victory,October, 2019

[120] Euonews: Opposition parties overturn Kosovo politics with election victory,October, 2019

What are the other key issues concerning voters?

With Europe's youngest population (the average age is 29), Kosovo has seen annual economic growth averaging 4% over the past decade, yet more than a third of people are unemployed[121].

Over 200,000 Kosovars have left their country and applied for asylum in the European Union since it declared independence, with Kosovo's population now at 1.8 million[122].

Securing a well-paid job often requires hard cash or political connections — indeed, it is this graft that frustrates a younger generation of Kosovars who are more likely to reject traditional parties.

"Young people born after the war understood the value of the liberation struggle, but the corruption that followed filled the pockets of ex-combatants. They can no longer find a job, can no longer have a visa to be able to emigrate and have insufficient services at home", Politi told Euronews[123].

"An important point for Kosovo will be to comply with EU criteria for the fight against corruption, which are well measurable: without this, young Kosovars will not be able to enjoy the system of facilitated visas to find work in the Schengen area," he added[124].

The lack of basic infrastructure is another issue of concern to voters.

"There are entire regions in which 40% of the population lives without sewage," said ISPI researcher Giorgio Fruscione.

7.3.What's the role of the diaspora?

Kosovo's diaspora is estimated between 700,000 and 800,000 people[125].

While Kosovars living abroad used to play an influential role in the country's politics, their influence appears to be fading.

This time, only 35,000 have registered to vote, Burjani told Euronews, adding that many were now older, second or third-generation immigrants and were "less and less connected to the daily life of Kosovo society[126]."

7.4.Who is in the running?

---

[121] Euonews: Opposition parties overturn Kosovo politics with election victory,October, 2019

[122] Agency for Statistic in Kosovo, Registration of population in 2011

[123] Euonews: Opposition parties overturn Kosovo politics with election victory,October, 2019

[124] Euonews: Opposition parties overturn Kosovo politics with election victory,October, 2019

[125] Euonews: Opposition parties overturn Kosovo politics with election victory,October, 2019

[126] Naim Rashiti ,Director,Euronews, October 2019

Dissatisfaction with the results delivered by Haradinaj's three-party governing coalition means more support is likely to go to opposition parties, with the Centre-right Democratic League for Kosovo (LDK) and the nationalist, left-leaning Vetevendosje competing for first place.

In the last elections in 2017, three former Kosovo Liberation Army leaders-turned-politicians, Haradinaj, Kadri Veseli and Fatmir Limaj formed the coalition, but this time they are standing separately.[127]

Vjosa Osmani, the LDK's candidate for prime minister, said she believed Kosovars were now ready to be led by a woman for the first time.[128]

Vjosa Osmani, leader of the Democratic League of Kosovo (LDK), speaks at a campaign rally in Suhareka, Kosovo, September 27, 2019. Picture taken September 27, 2019.REUTERS/Laura Hasani

"In more than 90% of cases, it is men who are involved in corruption. A woman sees the state and how to take care of our citizens completely differently," she told Reuters.

Osmani, along with Vetevendosje's Albin Kurti, is trying to harness anger over corruption to win votes.

Both are against making territorial concessions to Serbia.

7.5. What is the predicted result?

Opinion polls at the moment suggest no party will get enough support in Sunday's election to form a government, a result that is predicted to lead to prolonged coalition talks.

"The only coalition I can see forming is between the leftwing nationalists and LDK, if they find a consensus on a name," said Fruscione[129].

"The outcome is hard to predict and will largely depend on turnout," usually in proportional system is more complicated[130].

"Ruling parties are likely to lose against the opposition but we have to see how the coalition will be formed," he added[131].

---

[127] Euonews: Opposition parties overturn Kosovo politics with election victory,October, 2019

[128] LDK candidate for prime minister on election 2019

[129] Euronews,Fruscione,10.10.2019

[130] Proportional system, Election Law in Kosovo. http://www.gazetazyrtare.com/e-gov/index.php?option=com_content&task=view&id=157&Itemid=56&lang=en,10.09.2019

[131] Euronews,Fruscione,10.10.2019

7.6..EU observers in election, 6 October 2019

Well-administered and transparent elections affected by an uneven playing field, and marred by intimidation and lack of competition in the Kosovo Serb areas (Pristina, 8 October 2019)[132].

 The Chief Observer, Mrs Viola von Cramon-Taubadel, a Member of the European Parliament, presented today the preliminary findings of the European Union Election Observation Mission (EU EOM) on the 6 October early legislative elections in Kosovo[133].

"These early elections were well-administered and transparent. The campaign was vibrant and competitive allowing contestants to campaign freely in most of Kosovo." said Mrs von Cramon at a press conference in Pristina[134].

 The election day was orderly, and the EU observers positively assessed voting and counting. The Central Election Commission (CEC) ensured the transparency of the process by promptly publishing online preliminary unofficial results for political entities broken down by polling station. Mrs von Cramon added that "Transparency was a key feature of the CEC's work and it is commendable that despite the short time frame, the CEC has completed all electoral preparations on time[135]."The campaign environment in the Kosovo Serb areas was marred by intimidation, which targeted non-Srpska Lista candidates and supporters. Furthermore, misuse of public resources and a lack of transparency concerning campaign finance resulted in an uneven playing field throughout Kosovo[136].

"Recurring systemic problems with the election process identified also by previous observation missions such as provisions for calling early elections in a short timeframe, an unregulated pre-campaign period and others, need to be addressed in order to bring the election process in Kosovo fully in line with international standards for democratic elections. Said Mrs von Cramon, who also added that: "A set of recommendations presented together with the mission's Final Report will become truly meaningful only when given serious consideration in the next Assembly, and this should be done as soon as possible[137]."

Andrey Kovatchev, Head of the delegation from the European Parliament said: "We very much welcome the overall effective management of the process[138]. However, the issue of campaign finance is an area of ongoing concern that has been raised by previous observation missions. The regulatory framework does not ensure transparency

---

[132] EU observers in election, 6 October 2019

[133] EU observers in election, 6 October 2019

[134] EU observers in election, 6 October 2019

[135] EU observers in election, 6 October 2019

[136] EU observers in election, 6 October 2019

[137] EU observers in election, 6 October 2019

[138] EU observers in election, 6 October 2019

and integrity and it must be strengthened in order to fight corruption and guarantee a healthy   democracy."

On election day, the EU EOM deployed 108 observers from 27 EU Member States as well as Norway and Switzerland across Kosovo. The EU EOM will remain in Kosovo to follow the process at the Count and Results Centre and the resolution of any complaints and appeals, until the certification of final results[139].

7.7. Opposition parties beat 'war wing' in Kosovo elections

Opposition parties won the night in Kosovo's election Sunday taking the lead over former guerrillas who have dominated politics for the past decade. [140]

The leftist-nationalist Vetevendosje was in first place with 26 percent of the vote, followed by the centre-right LDK who had 25.2 percent after more than three quarters of the ballots were counted, the electoral commission said[141].But it is not still finale result.

The victory of the two opposition parties was a heavy rebuke to parties led by former guerrillas who battled Serbia in the 1990s, paving the way for Kosovo's independence.

"We did not win. We accept the verdict of the people and the PDK moves to the opposition," said Kadri Veseli, leader of the PDK party that has been in power since 2007 and is linked to President Hashim Thaçi.

With no camp taking an absolute majority, the opposition parties will need to unite to seal the PDK's place in the opposition.

While Vetevendosje and LDK have little overlap ideologically, they have already discussed the possibility of joining forces.

The party with the most votes will be tasked with forming the new government.

If the trend continues, it could be Vetevendosje's leader Albin Kurti, a 44-year-old who first gained fame as a student activist protesting Serbian repression in the 1990s before the war.

---

[139] EU observers in election, 6 October 2019

[140] EU observers in election, 6 October 2019

[141] France 24, Opposition parties beat 'war wing' in Kosovo elections

He has since become a strident critic of Kosovo's political elite, and his place at the helm would herald a new era for the young democracy.

Sunday's snap poll was called after ex-prime minister Ramush Haradinaj, a former guerrilla commander, resigned in July to face questioning by a special court in The Hague investigating war crimes from the 1998-99 separatist conflict with Serbia.

His party, which was allied with the PDK in the former government but this time ran alone, had one of the weaker showings with 11.6 percent.

The new leaders will now be under heavy pressure from the West to revive talks with Serbia.

The neighbours have yet to normalize ties two decades after they clashed in war, a lingering source of instability in Europe.

Kosovo, a former Yugoslav province, is recognized by most of the West but it needs Belgrade -- and its allies Russia and China -- to accept its statehood so it can get a seat in the United Nations.

Serbia is also under pressure to make peace with Kosovo in order to move forward with its EU accession process.

Yet their EU-led dialogue has been at a standstill for more than a year, with frequent diplomatic provocations souring efforts to build goodwill.

8.'Let them negotiate'

If the dialogue with Belgrade does resume, one of the most sensitive issues will be settling what powers to grant Serb-majority administrations in Kosovo.

There are approximately 40,000 Serbs living in the north and 80,000 scattered in and around a dozen enclaves in other parts of Kosovo, whose population is mainly ethnic Albanian.

<table>
<tr><td>Seats reserved for Serb in Kosovo Assembly

• Serbs have 10 reserved seats in parliament.</td></tr>
</table>

The Srpska Lista, which aligns with Belgrade, looked set for a landslide.

Speaking in Belgrade, Serbian President Aleksandar Vucic_said he would be ready to talk to Kurti's party if they are deemed the "legitimate representatives" of Kosovo[142].

8.1. Kosovo Voters Want a New Future, but Old Problems Linger

Ever since Kosovo ended its war with Serbia two decades ago, its dominant political figures have all been men who rose to prominence as fighters and held onto power despite failing to secure a lasting peace and presiding over a floundering economy.[143]

But in parliamentary elections on Sunday, a new generation of politicians offered them a serious challenge for the first time.[144] Opposition parties gained ground and the ruling party appeared to take a solid beating at the polls, according to Kosovo Election Commission projections based on 80 percent of votes counted on Sunday night[145].

While the bitter division with Serbia remains — the government in Belgrade refuses to recognize Kosovo as an independent nation — and hope for a rapprochement still far-off, observers hope that the vote might provide an opportunity for the country to shake off the corruption and mismanagement of the postwar years and focus on better governance[146].

At the vanguard of those challenging the entrenched leadership is Vjosa Osmani, 38, who grew up among the rubble-strewn ruins of her country, studied international law in the United States, then was elected to Parliament in 2011.[147]

Her party, the Democratic League, was running closely behind the nationalist Vetevendosje party led by Albin Kurti. The tight race — with no party likely to secure more than 30 percent of the vote — will likely set off a fierce competition for prime minister as coalitions are formed in coming weeks. If Ms. Osmani manages to secure power, she would become the country's first female prime minister. "It's important that Kosovo is represented by leaders who have risen in politics through merit, hard work and a resolve to do better," Ms. Osmani said in an interview on the eve of the election.

---

[142] New York Time, Kosovo Voters Want a New Future, but Old Problems Linger,October,2019

[143] New York Time, Kosovo Voters Want a New Future, but Old Problems Linger,October,2019

[144] New York Time, Kosovo Voters Want a New Future, but Old Problems Linger,October,2019

[145]Kosovo Voters Want a New Future, but Old Problems Linger
 New York Times , https://www.nytimes.com/2019/10/06/world/europe/kosovo-election-haradinaj-osmani.html

[146] Kosovo Voters Want a New Future, but Old Problems Linger
 New York Times , https://www.nytimes.com/2019/10/06/world/europe/kosovo-election-haradinaj-osmani.html

[147] Kosovo Voters Want a New Future, but Old Problems Linger
 New York Times , https://www.nytimes.com/2019/10/06/world/europe/kosovo-election-haradinaj-osmani.html

She said that some politicians of the war generation had "failed Kosovo citizens badly[148]."

While much of Eastern and Central Europe has undergone an economic boom in recent years, Kosovo has lagged far behind. Roughly one in four people in Kosovo are unemployed, wages remain among the lowest in Europe, corruption is rampant and organized crime is endemic.[149]

The early elections were called after Prime Minister Ramush Haradinaj resigned in July, - after being summoned to a court in The Hague for questioning about crimes against ethnic Serbs during and after the 1998-99 war. He served as an officer in the Kosovo Liberation Army at the time[150].

Despite having resigned, Mr. Haradinaj competed in Sunday's election. He seemed to have suffered a sound defeat.

As of Sunday night, Vetevendosje — or Self-Determination in English — was leading with 26 percent of the vote ahead of Ms. Osmani's party, which had 25 percent of votes.

The party of a former Parliament speaker, Kadri Veseli, an ally of Kosovo's president, Hashim Thaci, was third with 21 percent and far ahead of Mr. Thaci's longtime political rival, Mr. Haradinaj, who was a distant fourth with 11.5 percent of the vote[151].

Despite their differences, all the candidates know the public is angry, and all have vowed to root out corruption, to fight organized crime and nepotism and to lower unemployment[152]. They have promised to prioritize issues at home before yielding to pressure from the international community to negotiate with Serbia a final settlement on Kosovo's status. Serbia has so far blocked Kosovo from joining the United Nations and other international bodies, and five European Union states still decline to recognize it.[153]

---

[148]Kosovo Voters Want a New Future, but Old Problems Linger
 New York Times , https://www.nytimes.com/2019/10/06/world/europe/kosovo-election-haradinaj-osmani.html
[149] Kosovo Voters Want a New Future, but Old Problems Linger
 New York Times , https://www.nytimes.com/2019/10/06/world/europe/kosovo-election-haradinaj-osmani.html
[150]Kosovo Voters Want a New Future, but Old Problems Linger
 New York Times , https://www.nytimes.com/2019/10/06/world/europe/kosovo-election-haradinaj-osmani.html
[151] Kosovo Voters Want a New Future, but Old Problems Linger
 New York Times , https://www.nytimes.com/2019/10/06/world/europe/kosovo-election-haradinaj-osmani.html,6 October,2019
[152] Kosovo Voters Want a New Future, but Old Problems Linger
 New York Times , https://www.nytimes.com/2019/10/06/world/europe/kosovo-election-haradinaj-osmani.html,6 October,2019
[153] Kosovo Voters Want a New Future, but Old Problems Linger

A final settlement might also remove a barrier to Serbia one day becoming a member of the European Union[154].

"Again this is an opportunity for the older generation with old problems and old politicians to break the cycle of using Serbia as an excuse for the mistakes of Kosovo's governments. VV has leader in age 45, but this political party is consist by older people in presidency , the mayor body is leading by two people which was part of PDK.VV has electoral vote from people which are tired with other political party in Kosovo which they lead for 12 year with corruption, nepotism and without development of economy and health protection policy.

8.2.Decision on tariffs and dialogue : The first big test after the elections in Kosovo

Relations between Kosovo and Serbia, as well as Pristina's 100% tariffs on goods from Serbia and Bosnia and Herzegovina are major campaign themes ahead of the snap parliamentary elections in Kosovo, scheduled for 6 October.

The elections are taking place against the backdrop of international actors, such as Washington and Brussels, becoming increasingly explicit in their messages to Belgrade and Pristina, that the normalization talks must resume, and that the tariffs should be revoked quickly.

Political analist Kosovo and a member of the Balkans in Europe Policy Advisory Group (BiEPAG), stresses for *European Western Balkans* that the abolishing the tariffs and continuation of the dialogue with Serbia will be the first test of the new government after the elections, adding that such a decision will not be easy, especially since the condition for abolishing the tariffs may be that Serbia stops with the de-recognition campaign of Kosovo's independence and obstruction of Kosovo's membership in international organisations.

However, despite the potential political cost of the decision to revoke tariffs and resume the dialogue, election campaign and statements of the candidates for Prime Minister show that the will to pave the way to the solution exists nonetheless. Some of the political parties have so far proposed the removing the tariff and replacing it with reciprocity.

"*Vetëvendosje!* wants the reciprocity approach in which Kosovo will impose the same sanctions to those Serbia imposes toward Kosovo. Whereas, Democratic Party of Kosovo (PDK) is seemingly divided in this regard."

New York Times , https://www.nytimes.com/2019/10/06/world/europe/kosovo-election-haradinaj-osmani.html

[154] [154]Kosovo Voters Want a New Future, but Old Problems Linger

New York Times , https://www.nytimes.com/2019/10/06/world/europe/kosovo-election-haradinaj-osmani.html, 6 October ,2019

Democratic League of Kosovo (LDK) seems to have the most flexible approach toward the tariffs because many of the key party members have indicated that they are willing to suspend tariffs and constructively deal with the dialogue even yetis early to conclude.

On the other hand, political analysts emphasizes that some Kosovo's leaders, such as Ramush Haradinaj, promote a very risky agenda. Haradinaj is building his campaign on the "100% state" inspired by the 100% tariffs and against exchanging territories, his government has imposed.

Next Government   will address tariffs will surely be ready to deal with this fact.

"Election might affect the dialogue process depending on who will form the government. Yet, what the political scene has learned in the last two years is the need for consensus which goes beyond party lines", political parties after elections will have to work on consensus building new government.

8.3.A lukewarm approach to the EU

Dialogue with Serbia has been one of the main conditions for the progress on EU accession path of both countries and, even though the Committee for Civil Liberties, Justice and Home Affairs of the European Parliament reaffirmed its support for visa-free travel of the citizens of Kosovo last week, the process has been slow at best over the past two years.

Our interlocutors assess that, in spite of this, Kosovo's orientation remains towards the West. According to political analyst, public opinion, all political parties in Kosovo give their full support for the Euro-Atlantic agenda of the country.

"Good example of this support was recorded during the last Assembly's legislature when two of the biggest opposition parties were boycotting the proceedings of the Assembly due to the issues related to the Kosovo-Serbia dialogue, yet would come back and vote for EU related legislation".

However, during the current election campaign, the political parties are more cautious in promising visa liberalization or even setting a date for Kosovo's EU membership, which has been also a feature of the previous campaigns.

"Seemingly, the EU is not on the agenda. With the uncertainty surrounding the visa liberalization process citizen are mostly interested to happened soon , political parties in Kosovo are hesitate to include this issue in their programs" because nobody know is going to happened or not during 2019/20.

This has a lot to do with the lack of EU perspective, the sense of isolation, and the general understanding that the EU will not be politically able to deliver.

"The lack of delivery on the EU side might as well be used by the political elite to shift this attitude and re-define country's foreign strategic partners" in future .

The times of uncertainty, with the new External Action Service being led by a non-recognizer (Spain's Josep Borell), have contributed to the overall lukewarm approach of political parties toward EU integration process, with the only positive aspect being the lack of tendency to derail from EU or share negative approach or propaganda toward the Union, she concludes. Political parties they do not want the new negotiator come up from Spain with knowing reason.

8.4. Bullying Among Serbs Sours Kosovo's Democratic Gains

Last weekend's vote in Kosovo was widely seen as a democratic feather in the cap of Europe's newest state. But one stubborn problem for minority Serbs stuck out like a sore thumb.

MITROVICA, Kosovo -- When her father reached for the phone at around 6:45 p.m. on election night, he'd been content to sit out the October 6 voting along with the majority of Kosovo's 1.9 million registered voters. [155]

But within moments of hanging up, he was hurrying for the door, along with his wife, to the polling station in their majority-Serb community south of the Ibar River that remains a powerful symbol of Kosovo's ethnic divisions.

They had just 15 minutes before polling stations closed, the caller had told him bluntly, and he had to "do his civic duty."It was further evidence, said his daughter, who asked to remain anonymous, of the kind of pressure that they and other ethnic Serbs face across the country.

The pressure, she said, comes not from the ethnic Albanian majority but from other Serbs.

"He [rushed out to vote] because he works for Serbian institutions and fears jeopardizing his job because he didn't go to the polls," she told RFE/RL's Balkan Service. "My mother did the same."

8.5. Punching Above Its Weight

By hook or crook, the party that has controlled nearly all of the 10 seats in Kosovo's 120-seat parliament reserved for ethnic Serbs following each of the last two elections,

---

[155] CEC, https://www.kqz-ks.org/zgjedhjet-e-pergjithshme/zgjedhjet-per-kuvend-te-kosoves-2019/17.02.2021

Srpska Lista, punched above its weight again last week to take 6.6 percent of the national vote.

The **result** reflects strong turnout among ethnic Serbs, who are most densely concentrated north of the Ibar and are thought to make up some 1-2 percent of the national population.

By virtue of its place within each of Kosovo's last two governing coalitions and open support from the government of neighboring Serbia, which still doesn't recognize Kosovo's independence, Srpska Lista's influence extends well beyond mostly Serb communities.

But its methods have been publicly questioned by rival Serb politicians and by election monitors from the European Union, who warned on October 8 that campaigning had been "marred by intimidation, which targeted non-Srpska Lista candidates and supporters."

 The three other ethnic Serb parties in the running -- the Kosovar Serbs Party (0.2 percent), the Freedom coalition (0.12 percent), and the Independent Liberal Party (0.06 percent) -- failed to reach parliament by wide margins.[156]

"In the Kosovo Serb community, parties seeking to compete with Srpska Lista were unable to mount effective campaigns due in part to intimidation of candidates, their families and voters in general," the EU election-observation mission said in its preliminary statement.

"Srpska Lista-controlled municipalities, as well as the government of Serbia, directed Kosovo Serbs to vote only for Srpska Lista, while their opponents were denounced as anti-Serbian."

It was the bleakest aspect of a vote that was otherwise lauded as a major step forward for a still-partially recognized state and an example for others in the turbulent Balkans and beyond.

As a result, the EU observers said, "the electoral process for Kosovo Serbs fell short of...international standards.

"Rival Serb parties have repeatedly accused Srpska Lista itself of thuggery. Freedom (Sloboda) coalition leader Nenad Rasic, at a debate alongside two other Serb party leaders in Caglavica, alleged Srpska Lista intimidation that included the "interrogation" of the wife of a coalition activist and a warning that she would lose her job.

---

[156] CEC,https://www.kqz-ks.org/zgjedhjet-e-pergjithshme/zgjedhjet-per-kuvend-te-kosoves-2019/

He told RFE/RL's Balkan Service that the intensifying tactics to boost Srpska Lista's support -- including from Belgrade -- since that party's creation six years ago was an attack on self-determination for Kosovar Serbs.

They have imposed the standard that 'whoever is not with us is against us, and whoever is against us is our enemy,'" Rasic said, calling it "a step further" than past behavior.

Elsewhere, Rasic suggested his own life might be in danger.

8.6. Alleged Intimidation

Prosecutors in Kosovo were said to be looking into a number of cases of alleged intimidation. Srpska Lista declined to respond to RFE/RL's Balkan Service questions about such allegations.

In 2018, a prominent entrepreneur and influential political voice for Serb-Kosovar dialogue, Oliver Ivanovic, was shot dead outside his party's offices in the predominantly Serb portion of the northern city of Mitrovica[157].

The killing hasn't been solved, but reports say a senior official within Srpska List is wanted for questioning. Meanwhile Ivanovic's former party, the SDP Citizens Initiative, announced in September that it was teaming up with Srpska Lista for the October 6 elections[158].

Based in Mitrovica, Srpska List was created ahead of national elections in 2014, when it garnered about 38,000 votes. In this month's balloting it received more than 52,000 votes, upward of half of the best estimates of Kosovo's entire ethnic Serb population[159].

Its results are watched eagerly in the Serbian capital, where President Aleskandar Vucic has unapologetically stumped for Srpska Lista.

Speculation that the party somehow takes its marching orders from Belgrade are difficult to prove, but the relationship is clearly close.

The EU observation mission noted that "the government of Serbia and the local authorities in the Serb-majority municipalities strongly directed Kosovo Serbs to vote only for Srpska Lista."

The observers cited reports of Serbian officials being turned away at Kosovo's border during the 10-day campaign ahead of the snap elections.

---

[157] Balkan Insight,October,2019

[158] Balkan Insight, October,2019

[159] Balkan Insight,October,2019

Isidora Stakic, a researcher at the Belgrade Security Policy Center, told RFE/RL recently that their research from February "shows that Serbs living in northern Kosovo are more afraid of representatives of the Serbian authorities than of Albanians."

The "greatest pressure," she said, is from Srpska Lista and its Serbian government allies.

Serbia's president, Aleskandar Vucic, welcomed the October 6 results by saying Srpska Lista had "won its most convincing victory in its history," according to Balkan Insight, adding, "This is one of my favorite wins because it happened under the most difficult conditions[160]."

Many international observers are keen to see any new government in Pristina beat a speedy path to renewed talks with Serbia over normalizing relations between the two ex-Yugoslav neighbors[161].

Those negotiations have been on hold since Vucic abandoned them after Kosovo announced a 100-percent tariff on Serbian imports in November. Their outcome could clear the way for UN recognition for Kosovo, whose statehood is recognized by more than 110 countries but not by Serbia, Russia, China, or Spain, for instance.[162]

The two leading parties in the October 6 elections -- the pro-Albanian Self-Determination party and the Democratic League -- kicked off talks on a possible coalition on October 10.[163]

The EU election observer's mission urged Kosovo's parliament to give the Serb intimidation and other problems "serious consideration...as soon as possible."

Albin Kurti, the leader of Kosovo's leftist Vetevendosje (Self-Determination) party that won a plurality of votes in parliamentary elections, said that dialogue with Serbia has to include the "recognition of Kosovo's independence." Speaking to RFE/RL on October 10 in Pristina, the country's likely future prime minister also said that unless Serbia faces its past, there would be no peace and reconciliation. PRISTINA -- Kosovo's leftist-nationalist Vetevendosje (Self-Determination) party and the center-right Democratic League of Kosovo (LDK) have started coalition talks following this weekend's general elections.

"Without wasting time we have started talks with the common idea of a more efficient government and a stronger state," Vetevendosje leader Albin Kurti said on October 10, adding that the expectations of Kosovo's citizens are "very high."

---

[160] Balkan Insight,October,2019
[161] Balkan Insight,October,2019
[162] Balkan Insight,October,2019
[163] Balkan Insight,October,2019

LDK's prime minister candidate, , said that, during their first meeting, the two parties "showed goodwill to govern together and goodwill to work in the interest of citizens."

LDK candidate for PM said they would wait until the final election results before reaching an agreement.

VV and LDK said the parties discussed reducing the number of ministers and deputy ministers.

According to final preliminary results, Vetevendosje garnered 25.5 percent of the vote in the October 6 snap elections, followed by LDK with 24.8 percent there is not final result.[164]

The former ruling party, the Democratic Party of Kosovo (PDK), which has dominated politics for more than a decade, placed third, while the coalition of outgoing Prime Minister Ramush Haradinaj's Alliance for the Future of Kosovo was fourth.

8.7. Turnout was 44.5 percent[165]

EU observers said the polls were "well-administered and transparent," but pointed out shortcomings including the "intimidation" of ethnic Serbs by the main political force that represents the country's Serb minority[166].

The early elections were triggered by Haradinaj's resignation in July after war crimes prosecutors at The Hague summoned him for questioning over his wartime role as a commander of the Kosovo Liberation Army (UCK)[167].

The election campaign was dominated by issues of corruption, high unemployment, and a possible peace deal with Serbia, which has not recognized from 116 international stats.

Kosovo remains very poor, with unemployment at 25 percent. More than 200,000 Kosovars have left and applied for asylum in the European Union since Pristina declared independence in 2008[168].

8.8. Kosovo Election Winner Not In Hurry To Renew Serbia Talks

---

[164] CEC, https://www.kqz-ks.org/zgjedhjet-e-pergjithshme/zgjedhjet-per-kuvend-te-kosoves-2019/

[165] CEC, https://www.kqz-ks.org/zgjedhjet-e-pergjithshme/zgjedhjet-per-kuvend-te-kosoves-2019/

[166] Balkan Insight,October,2019

[167] Balkan Insight,October,2019

[168] Balkan Insight,October,2019

The leader of the center-left party that won a plurality of votes in Kosovo's early parliamentary elections on October 6 says he isn't hankering to restart formal talks designed to normalize relations with neighboring Serbia.[169]

In an interview with the Associated Press published on October 8, Vetevendosje party chief Albin Kurti, who is poised to become the next prime minister, said that Pristina-Belgrade negotiations aren't currently at the top of his list of things to do[170]."It cannot be top priority on day one of me as a new prime minister," he said.

His party defeated center-right groupings that were formed by former fighters from the Kosovo Liberation Army who had been in power for more than a decade.

Kosovo declared independence from Serbia in 2008 after a decade of fighting an insurgent war amid a crackdown by former Serbian leader Slobodan Milosevic.

Serbia, China, Russia and five European Union countries don't recognize Kosovo's statehood, although more than 117 countries do.

Dialogue between Serbia and Kosovo started in 2011, but has since stalled. A bone of contention includes a 100 percent tariff on Serbian goods[171].

"Only after the principle of reciprocity has been put in place, [then] we can lift the tariffs," Kurti told AP, referring to 33 deals signed between Kosovo and Serbia[172].

Both the EU's probable future foreign-policy chief, Josep Borrell, and the new U.S. special envoy to Kosovo-Serbia, Richard Grenell, have stated that normalizing relations between the neighboring countries is a priority.[173]

Until tensions defuse and relations stabilize, the EU has said prospects of Kosovo and Serbia joining the 28-member bloc remain dim.[174]

Kurti is scheduled to meet Grenell, currently the U.S. ambassador to Germany, on October 9.[175]

8.9. 'First True Transition': Key Takeaways From Kosovo's Watershed Vote

---

[169] Balkan Insight,October,2019

[170] Kosovo Election 2019, Radio Free Europe, https://www.rferl.org/z/679,10.11.2019
[171] Kosovo Election 2019, Radio Free Europe, https://www.rferl.org/z/679,10.11.2019
[172] Kosovo Election 2019, Radio Free Europe, https://www.rferl.org/z/679,10.11.2019
[173] Kosovo Election 2019, Radio Free Europe, https://www.rferl.org/z/679,10.11.2019
[174] Kosovo Election 2019, Radio Free Europe, https://www.rferl.org/z/679,10.11.2019
[175] Kosovo Election 2019, Radio Free Europe, https://www.rferl.org/z/679,10.11.2019

Kurti, who spent 2 ½ years in a Serbian prison for his pro-independence actions, has already sparked the ire of Belgrade.

When asked about a ethnic-Serbian minister in his future government, a constitutional requirement, Kurti said he preferred "a Serb minister who comes from those Serbs who recognize the independence of Kosovo."

This prompted a furious reaction from Belgrade with Marko Djuric, the Serbian official in charge of Kosovar affairs, accusing Kurti of being an "extremist" who was "stomping" on the democratic rights of Kosovo-Serbs.

Following the elections, Kurti's Vetevendosje party asked the center-right Democratic League of Kosovo (LDK) to form a coalition government.[176]

EU observers say Kosovo's elections were "well-administered and transparent," but pointed out shortcomings including the "intimidation" of ethnic Serbs by the main political force that represents the country's Serb minority -- the Belgrade-backed Serb List party.[177]

It won the 10 seats in Kosovo's 120-seat legislature that are reserved for ethnic Serbs.[178]

 European Union observers say Kosovo's parliamentary elections were "well-administered and transparent," but pointed out shortcomings including the "intimidation" of ethnic Serbs by the main party representing the country's Serb minority[179].

According to nearly-final preliminary results, the leftist-nationalist Vetevendosje won the October 6 snap elections, but the party did not garner enough votes to rule on its own and is expected to enter coalition talks with the center-right Democratic League of Kosovo (LDK).

The head of the EU Election Observation Mission, European Parliament member Viola von Cramon-Taubadel, presented the preliminary findings of the mission on October 8, saying the campaign was "vibrant and competitive" while election day was "orderly[180]."

However, the campaign environment in the Kosovo Serb areas was "marred by

---

[176] Kosovo Election 2019, Radio Free Europe, https://www.rferl.org/z/679,10.11.2019
Kosovo Election 2019, Radio Free Europe, https://www.rferl.org/z/679,10.11.2019
[177] Constitution of Republic of Kosovo
[178] Kosovo Election 2019, Radio Free Europe, https://www.rferl.org/z/679,10.11.2019
[179] Kosovo Election 2019, Radio Free Europe, https://www.rferl.org/z/679,10.11.2019
[180] Kosovo Election 2019, Radio Free Europe, https://www.rferl.org/z/679,10.11.2019

intimidation, which targeted non-Srpska Lista candidates and supporters," a statement said.

"Misuse of public resources and a lack of transparency concerning campaign finance resulted in an uneven playing field throughout Kosovo," it added.

With more than 99 percent of the ballots counted, results from the Central Election Commission showed Vetevendosje garnered 25.5 percent of the vote followed by LDK with 24.8 percent.[181]

The former ruling party, the Democratic Party of Kosovo (PDK), which has dominated politics for more than a decade, placed third with 21.2[182] percent of the vote, while the coalition of outgoing Prime Minister Ramush Haradinaj's Alliance for the Future of Kosovo had 11.5[183] percent.

The turnout was 44 percent, a slight improvement on the previous election two years ago.[184]

Vetevendosje's leader, former student protest leader Albin Kurti, pledged on October 7 to work quickly to try and form a coalition government with LDK, whose prime ministerial candidate is Vjosa Osmani.

9.Urging Reforms

In a joint statement, EU foreign policy chief Federica Mogherini and Enlargement Commissioner Johannes Hahn urged the upcoming government to "swiftly resume work on reforms in support of economic and social development as well as rule of law, on the implementation of the EU-Kosovo Stabilization and Association Agreement and on the EU-facilitated Dialogue with Belgrade."[185]

Mogherini and Hahn said they "expect all political actors to remain committed to these processes, which are key for Kosovo's future, for progress on its European path, and most importantly for the benefit of the people of Kosovo and of the whole region."[186]

The early election was triggered by Haradinaj's resignation in July after war crimes

---

[181] CEC,https://www.kqz-ks.org/zgjedhjet-e-pergjithshme/zgjedhjet-per-kuvend-te-kosoves-2019/

[182] CEC,https://www.kqz-ks.org/zgjedhjet-e-pergjithshme/zgjedhjet-per-kuvend-te-kosoves-2019/

[183] CEC,https://www.kqz-ks.org/zgjedhjet-e-pergjithshme/zgjedhjet-per-kuvend-te-kosoves-2019/

[184]CEC, https://www.kqz-ks.org/zgjedhjet-e-pergjithshme/zgjedhjet-per-kuvend-te-kosoves-2019/

[185] Kosovo Election 2019, Radio Free Europe, https://www.rferl.org/z/679,10.11.2019

[186] Kosovo Election 2019, Radio Free Europe, https://www.rferl.org/z/679,10.11.2019

prosecutors at The Hague summoned him for questioning over his wartime role as a commander of the Kosovo Liberation Army (UCK)[187].

The election campaign was dominated by the issues of corruption, high unemployment, and a possible peace deal with Serbia that would clear the way for Kosovo's membership in the United Nations[188].

Kosovo's independence has been recognized by more than 117 states but not by others, including five EU members, as well as Serbia, Russia, and China.

European Union-sponsored talks aimed at normalizing ties between Pristina and Belgrade stalled last year over Kosovo's decision to impose a 100 percent tax on goods from Serbia.

Kosovo has Europe's youngest population with an average age of 29, and economic growth has averaged 4 percent over the past decade. But it remains very poor -- unemployment is 25 percent -- and more than 200,000 Kosovars have left and applied for asylum in the European Union since Pristina won its independence.[189]

9.1. Kosovo holds election amid calls for resuming Serbia talks…

 Kosovo is holding an early general election Sunday amid calls for leaders to resume dialogue with Serbia over normalizing ties.

The vote comes after the outgoing prime minister resigned following a request from a Hague-based court to question him over crimes against ethnic Serbs during and after the country's 1998-99 war[190].

The election will be Kosovo's seventh since the end of the war, and 1.9 million people are eligible to cast ballots to elect 120 lawmakers.

Kosovo's 2008 independence from Serbia has been recognized by more than 116 countries but not by Belgrade. European Union-sponsored talks aimed at normalizing ties between the two countries stalled last year over Kosovo's decision to impose a 100% tax on goods from Serbia.[191]

Other issues in the election include bringing down the unemployment rate which stands at more than 25%, organized crime and corruption.[192] No single political party is likely to

---

[187]Kosovo Election 2019, Radio Free Europe, https://www.rferl.org/z/679,10.11.2019

[188] Kosovo Election 2019, Radio Free Europe, https://www.rferl.org/z/679,10.11.2019

[189] Kosovo holds election amid calls for resuming Serbia talks/Washington Post

[190] Kosovo holds election amid calls for resuming Serbia talks/Washington Post
Kosovo holds election amid calls for resuming Serbia talks/Washington Post

[191] Kosovo holds election amid calls for resuming Serbia talks/Washington Post

[192] Kosovo holds election amid calls for resuming Serbia talks/Washington Post

win the vote on its own and coalitions have always proved hard to form and easy to fall apart.

The outgoing Prime Minister, Ramush Haradinaj, having been questioned in The Hague but not charged, is standing for re-election with his Alliance for Kosovo Future. He faces Vjosa Osmani of the Democratic League of Kosovo, the first-ever female candidate for prime minister in the country; Kadri Veseli of the Democratic Party of Kosovo; and Albin Kurti of the Self-Determination Movement Party, which has used extreme methods like throwing tear gas and water bottles in parliament to protest against deals with Serbia.[193]

All candidates except Osmani are former fighters of the Kosovo Liberation Army, which triggered the 1998-1999 war that ended when NATO intervened on behalf of the Albanian majority[194].

Kosovo's relations with Serbia have soured further recently after Haradinaj set a 100% tariff on Serb and Bosnian goods last year as a way to get Serbia to recognize Kosovo and to end efforts to prevent it from participating in international organizations.

All political parties, except for Haradinaj's and one closely allied to him, have criticized the tariff. Fearing a loss of votes, none has explicitly said they would lift or suspend it and resume talks, despite pressure from the U.S. and EU.

Instead, Osmani and Kurti say the tariff should be replaced with reciprocity in the application of 33 agreements signed with Belgrade since 2011.

"That was a perfectly legitimate measure although it was done for the wrong reasons," LDK said.

"The majority of political parties are clear in their stance to continue the dialogue, to stick to the international partners' requests," says Evliana Berani, editor-in-chief of Infoglob, an independent online media page. "I am sure each party will start from the beginning to deal with the tax[195]."

Though there are no reliable polls before voting, it is believed by political observers that the opposition may have the upper hand because Osmani and Kurti haven't been embroiled in widespread corruption scandals.[196]

Trade, retail and construction are the main sectors of the economy and the industrial sector is weak. The country also has a strong dependence on remittances from the

---

[193] Kosovo holds election amid calls for resuming Serbia talks/Washington Post
[194] Kosovo holds election amid calls for resuming Serbia talks/Washington Post
[195] Evliana Berani, editor-in-chief of Infoglob
[196] IPKZH,Curuption in Kosovo,12.02.2021

diaspora, mainly in Germany and Switzerland, which has reached up to 14% of gross domestic product.[197]

"Kosovo is at a crossroads, with high level of unemployment and poverty, with high level of migration and a pessimistic sentiment of the people," says Berani, convinced that whoever wins the election "will be forced to change drastically the way Kosovo is governed. People are tired of 'major' ideas."

The Serb minority, with 10 seats in the 120-seat parliament, remains a key player in Kosovo, especially since their votes may be needed in a coalition to form a Cabinet, a scenario that occurred two years ago.

The Belgrade-backed Srpska Lista, or Serb List, group is expected to garner the most votes in the Serb-run part of the country amid a fierce campaign that calls for Serb unity. Ten other seats belong to different minorities.

The European Union has sent a 61-member team of observers for the election to show that Pristina "remains a political priority."

9.2. West tells Kosovo and Serbia to return to negotiating table

Four European countries and the United States urged Kosovo and Serbia on Tuesday to re-launch their dialogue on normalizing ties in order to advance their bid for EU membership. [198]

The EU-sponsored dialogues between Belgrade and Pristina was halted last November when Kosovo introduced a 100 percent tax on goods produced in Serbia, pledging to remove it only when Belgrade recognizes Kosovo as a sovereign state. [199]

"The status quo prevents progress on Kosovo's and Serbia's path toward the European Union (EU) and is simply not sustainable," said the so-called Quint group of the United States, Italy, France, Germany and Britain.

They urged both parties to remove obstacles for a dialogue first.

"For Kosovo, that means suspending the tariffs imposed on Serbia. For Serbia, that means suspending the de-recognition campaign against Kosovo," a joint statement said. [200]

Kosovo, with a 90 percent ethnic Albanian majority, declared independence from Serbia in 2008, nearly 10 years after NATO bombing drove Serb forces out of the country. It

---

[197] Kosovo holds election amid calls for resuming Serbia talks/Washington Post
[198] Kosovo holds election amid calls for resuming Serbia talks/Washington Post
[199] Kosovo holds election amid calls for resuming Serbia talks/Washington Post
[200] Kosovo holds election amid calls for resuming Serbia talks/Washington Post

has been recognized by 117 states but not by five EU member states, Serbia and Russia.

Serbia still considers Kosovo part of its territory and has blocked Pristina's membership in international organizations including Interpol and UNESCO. It has also asked some countries to revert their decision to recognize Kosovo as a sovereign state. Marko Djuric who is the head of the Serbian government's Office for Kosovo said the five countries that wrote the letter were in favor of unconditional recognition of Kosovo.

He said that Serbia had acknowledged the letter but that "the policy toward Kosovo will be guided by interests".

Pristina's new official negotiating team for talks with Belgrade in Brussels has agreed what it calls a 'Dialogue Platform' for negotiations on a final and legally-binding agreement on the normalization of relations with Serbia – including a demand that Belgrade pledges to recognize Kosovo.[201]

The negotiating platform, which BIRN has seen, was delivered to parliament speaker Kadri Veseli on Friday and will soon be put to a vote in the legislature.

The first principle agreed by the negotiators says that Kosovo's main goal is to obtain recognition from Serbia with four legally binding promises, including the dropping of Belgrade's objections to Kosovo joining the UN.[202]

The platform document says that Pristina wants "the halting of all activities that hinder Kosovo on the journey towards its international recognition as an independent and sovereign country; the respecting of the territorial sovereignty and integrity of the Republic of Kosovo; the halting of objections, or the encouraging of third parties to object to, the application of the Republic of Kosovo to join international organizations, including the UN, the Council of Europe, the OSCE, and their agencies; and giving up all forms of interference in the internal matters or international relations of the Republic of Kosovo".[203]

The platform insists that a final deal with Belgrade must include an agreement to establish a new tribunal "for the investigation, prosecution and adjudication of war crimes committed by Serbia in Kosovo in 1998 and 1999".[204]

The suggestion of a new court to try Serbs comes as the Kosovo Specialist Chambers, a Hague-based tribunal set up to try former Kosovo Liberation Army guerrillas and others for wartime crimes in Kosovo, prepares to issue its first indictments.

---

[201] Kosovo holds election amid calls for resuming Serbia talks/Washington Post
[202] Kosovo holds election amid calls for resuming Serbia talks/Washington Post
[203] Kosovo holds election amid calls for resuming Serbia talks/Washington Post
[204] Kosovo holds election amid calls for resuming Serbia talks/Washington Post

The Kosovo negotiators' platform also says that issues like wartime missing persons, victims of wartime sexual violence and reparations for war damage should become part of the negotiations with Serbia.

The platform includes a further principle which states that the territory of Kosovo shall not be altered.

Kosovo's President Hashim Thaci caused controversy last year when he suggested that there might be a "border correction" with Serbia as part of a final deal to normalise relations.

The issue caused a serious rift between Thaci and Prime Minister Ramush Haradinaj, who strongly opposes any border changes such as an exchange of territory with Serbia.

After delivering the platform to the parliament speaker, the joint leader of the negotiation team, Fatmir Limaj, urged MPs to adopt it.

"The principles are ones that guarantee peace in this part of the region. Everyone should get it clear that Kosovo is going to Brussels for recognition, nothing else," Limaj told media.[205]

According to the platform, the final agreement between Pristina and Belgrade will enter into force only after "a) Serbia has recognised Kosovo, b) a referendum for the agreement has been held in Kosovo, and c) the agreement is ratified by the parliaments of the two countries".[206]

Serbia has vowed never to recognize its former province as independent.

Talks between officials from Pristina and Belgrade have been ongoing in Brussels since 2013, and a successful outcome is seen as crucial to both countries' hopes of joining the EU.[207]

However the talks are currently suspended amid a row over Kosovo's imposition of import taxes on Serbian goods.

---

[205] Kosovo holds election amid calls for resuming Serbia talks/Washington Post
[206] Kosovo holds election amid calls for resuming Serbia talks/Washington Post
[207] Kosovo holds election amid calls for resuming Serbia talks/Washington Post

Conclusions:

Electoral reform should take place in two directions: the technical reform of electoral rules was easier and the reform of the electoral system, while this reform is more difficult to happen, that is, the reform of the electoral system. The reform of the electoral system in semi-majority would have a positive effect on the efficiency government in the state and in strengthening responsibility. Conditional voting should be removed, it is completely unnecessary, as well as voting by mail should be removed, and replaced by voting in the embassies of the state of Kosovo. Dissatisfied with the work of governments for a while long time in Kosovo has influenced the decrease in participation in elections among citizens, but in 2021 there were more participants, about 47%[208]. The reasons for the increase in the electorate for going to the elections came as a result of a long period of government degradation in the state of Kosovo by the political parties LDK, PDK, AAKAKR, but even now that a new political entity VV has come to power, it has also started disappointment grows in Kosovo, due to the many problems that burden the state from economic, social to education and justice. Let us remind that the law on elections at both levels does not specify the validity of the electoral process based on the participation of the electorate through setting a percentage or quota of citizens' participation in elections. The last changes in the law for the general elections were few and more technical, the agreement between the parties was made in advance. The new law foresees the voting of citizens outside Kosovo by post and in the Embassy of Kosovo. As well as the right of those who vote until 10 candidates in the election list.

Depoliticization of electoral institutions as follows: The CEC, the MEC and the PSC must take place through a legal reform system, the CEC must be composed of judges and academics who are independent of politics. These three institutions must be completely depoliticized in order to the elections are administered correctly and without abuses and without legal violations.

It is of great importance that these three institutions are completely depoliticized as follows:

    1. Central Election Commission (CEC) -
    2.Municipal Election Commissions (MECs)
    3. Polling Station Councils (PSCs)

---

[208] Douch Welle , **LVV fitoi më së shumti vota në zgjedhjet parlamentare në Kosovë**

Without the change of the Law on Elections, this depoliticization of decision-making in the CEC cannot happen, so the trend of control of political parties in the CEC will continue. Article 59, Article 61, of the Law on General Elections should be amended.

Municipal Election Commissions should also be depoliticized by replacing them with civil servants so that decision-making is completely depoliticized, in this regard should be amended Article 67.69 of the Law on General Elections. And in the end the counting of votes should be depoliticized, it should be done by civil servants. To make this passible should be amended Article 74, Article 75 of the Law on General Elections.

Political parties in favor of an impartial, credible electoral process must agree on the legal reform of the General Law to achieve high quality standards based on the standards set by ODIR.

- The counting of candidate's votes by their parties is one of the main problems that damage the process of organizing elections and cause significant problems in the evaluation of international observer organizations in Kosovo such as the EU, the Council of Europe, the OSCE and others.

Political parties in Kosovo must agree on the DE- politicization of electoral bodies because DE- politicization also has a positive effect on the organization, administration, counting and announcement of valid results for candidates in the open proportional list in Kosovo.

The votes of the parties and their candidates must be counted by the civil servants.

Political parties must accept the division into constituencies in Kosovo, so Kosovo must have at least 6 constituencies.

The CEC, even without changing the existing law, can improve the rule for counting the votes so that the votes, especially of the candidates, are counted faster and more efficiently, with greater control of the CEC and greater monitoring by international monitory organizations.

The DE politicization of the CEC, the MEC, the PSC must take place through a comprehensive electoral reform.

Literatura:

Blerim Burjani, Reforma Zgjedhore, Instituti i Kosovës për Zhvillimin e Politikave (IKPD), Prishtinë,2014

.Blerim Burjani, Interpretimi i së Drejtës, Instituti i Kosovës për Zhvillimin e Politikave (IKPD), Prishtinë, 2011
Daan Everst, Review of the OSCE mission in Kosovo's activities 1999-2001

Douche Welle, Kosovë: Shpallen rezultatet përfundimtare të zgjedhjeve, Douche Welle

Këshilli i Evropës, Misioni Vëzhgues Kosovë , Zgjedhjet e Përgjithshme, Tetor 2004

Ligji për Zgjedhjet e Përgjithshme të Republikës së Kosovës

Ligji për Zgjedhjet Lokale të Republikës së Kosovës

Karta e Këshillit të Evropës për Vetadministrim Lokal

Komisioni Qendror Zgjedhor , https://web1.kqz-ks.org/rregullat-zgjedhore/

Vezhguesit e zgjedhjeve , https://www .kqz-ks.org/zgjedhjet-e-pergjithshme/zgjedhjet-per-kuvend-te-kosoves-2019/

Raporti I Vezhgimit te Zgjedhjeve, Zgjedhjet per Kuvendin e Kosoves, http://demokracianeveprim.org/ë p-content/uploads/2019/12/DnV_RAPORTI-I-V%C3%8BZHGIMIT-T%C3%8B-ZGJEDHJEVE.pdf,2019

Rezultatet preliminare të zgjedhjeve - VV e para https://ë ë ë .dë .com/sq/rezultatet-preliminare-t%C3%AB-zgjedhjeve-vv-e-para/a-50718777

Misioni I Bashkimit Evropian per Vezhgimin e Zgjedhjeve ,Raporti Perfundimtar ,Kosove 2014

Manual për Ndjekjen e Zbatimit të Rekomandimeve për Zgjedhjet -Gjetjet kryesore të Raportit 2020 për Kosovën, https: //ec.europa.eu /commission/presscorner/detail/en/COUNTRY_20_1797

.Mbështetje për zgjedhjet në Ballkanin Perëndimor, 19.Komisioni Qendror i Zgjedhjeve

MATERIAL DISKUTIMI PËR PROCESIN ZGJEDHOR, http://ëëë.mei-ks.net/repository/docs/Material_Diskutues_Procesi_Zgjedhor.pdf

Literature:

1.Blerim Burjani, Electoral   Reform, Institute of Kosovo for Policy Development (IKPD), Pristina,2014

2.Blerim Burjani, Interpretation of Law, Institute of Kosovo for Policy Development (IKPD),, Pristina, 2011

3.Douche Welle , Kosovo: The final results of the elections are announced, Douche Welle

4.Council of Europe, Observation Mission KOSOVO, General Election, October 2004

5.Law on General Elections of Republic of Kosovo

6.Law on Local Election Of Republic Kosovo

7.Law on Constitutional Court of Slovenia

8..Law on Constitutional Court of Croatia

9.Law on Constitutional Court of Montenegro

10.Law on Constitutional Court of Serbia

11.ZGJEDHJET E PARAKOHSHME PËR KUVENDIN E REPUBLIKËS SË   KOSOVËS 2019, https://www.kqz-ks.org/zgjedhjet-e-pergjithshme/zgjedhjet-per-kuvend-te-kosoves-2019/ezhguesit

12.Vezhguesit e zgjedhjeve , https://www.kqz-ks.org/zgjedhjet-e-pergjithshme/zgjedhjet-per-kuvend-te-kosoves-2019/

.13. Raporti I Vezhgimit te Zgjedhjeve, Zgjedhjet për Kuvendin e Kosovës, http://demokracianeveprim.org/wp-content/uploads/2019/12/DnV_RAPORTI-I-V%C3%8BZHGIMIT-T%C3%8B-ZGJEDHJEVE.pdf,2019

14.Rezultatet preliminare të zgjedhjeve - VV e para https://www.dw.com/sq/rezultatet-preliminare-t%C3%AB-zgjedhjeve-vv-e-para/a-50718777

15.Zyra e OSBE-së për Institucione Demokratike dhe të Drejtat e Njeriut Misioni për Vëzhgimin e Zgjedhjeve Republika e Maqedonisë së Veriut Zgjedhjet e parakohshme parlamentare, 12 prill 2020 RAPORT I PËRKOHSHËM 3 - 31 mars 2020,https://www.osce.org/files/f/documents/2/3/451369.pdf15.

16.Misioni I Bashkimit Evropian per Vezhgimin e Zgjedhjeve ,Raporti Perfundimtar ,Kosove 2014

17. Manual për Ndjekjen e Zbatimit të Rekomandimeve për Zgjedhjet -Key findings of th 2020 Report on Kosovo,https: //ec.europa.eu /commission/presscorner/detail/en/COUNTRY_20_1797

18.Support to Elections in the Western Balkans, OSCE/ ODIR,https://www.osce.org/files/f/documents/4/9/383574.pdf,

19. **KOSOVO* MAYORAL AND MUNICIPAL ASSEMBLY ELECTIONS, EUROPEAN UNION ELECTION OBSERVATION MISSION , FINAL REPORT, 22 OCTOBER 2017**

20. EU Election Observation Mission Report Mentions KWN's Campaign . https://womensnetwork.org/eu-election-observation-mission-report-mentions-kwns-campaign/

<u>21.</u> **The Case of Kosovo: From "International Statebuilding" to an "Internationally Supervised and Independent Country"**https://www.cairn.info/revue-l-europe-en-formation-2008-3-page-189.htm

22. **ELECTORAL AND PARTY SYSTEM IN KOSOVO A PERSPECTIVE OF INTERNAL PARTY DEMOCRACY DEVELOPMENT**

23. The International Foundation for Electoral Systems (IFES) , SELECTING A MODEL FOR ELECTION ADMINISTRATION IN KOSOVO: CONCLUSIONS & RECOMMENDATIONS FROM DISCUSSION FORUM AND CONFERENCE HELD ON 1-2 AND 16 FEBRUARY 2002

24. The International Foundation for Electoral Systems (IFES) ,Supporting the CECandECAP,https://www.ifes.org/kosovo?type%5Belection_faq%5D=election_faq&type%5Belection_material%5D=election_material&type%5Bmultimedia%5D=multimedia&type%5Bnews_and_updates%5D=news_and_updates&type%5Bpublication%5D=publication&type%5Bsurvey%5D=survey&page=6

25. **Bjørg Hope Galtung, KOSOVO: ASSEMBLY ELECTIONS OCTOBER 2004, Report.**

26. United Nations,Recent Kosovo Election Marks Most Significant Change to Political Landscape in 12 Years, Special Representative Tells Security Council, https://www.un.org/press/en/2019/sc14008.doc.htm

27. **NDI,Ksovo Public Opinion Poll 2020, https: //www.ndi.org /publications/ndi-kosovo-public-opinion-poll-2020**

28. Beáta Huszka.The power of perspective: Why EU membership still matters in the Western Balkans

29. Laura Wise and Timofey Agarin, **European style electoral politics in an ethnically divided society. The case of Kosovo, https: //www. degruyter.com /view/journals /soeu/65/1/article-p99.xml**

30. EUROPEAN UNION ELECTION OBSERVATION MISSION TO KOSOVO FOR EARLY PARLIAMENTARY ELECTIONS, POSSIBLE TENTATIVE ELECTION DATES 22 OR 29 SEPTEMBER, OR 06 OCTOBER 2019.

31<u>Elton Tota</u>.EU recommendations on the future elections in Kosovo, https://balkaneu.com/eu-recommendations-on-the-future-elections-in-kosovo/, 12/09/2017

32. <u>Elton Tota</u>.EU recommendations on the future elections in Kosovo, https://balkaneu.com/eu-recommendations-on-the-future-elections-in-kosovo/, 12/09/2017

Printed by Books on Demand GmbH, Norderstedt / Germany